金融英文700選

砺波 元 [著]

一般社団法人 金融財政事情研究会

■はじめに

　本書は、金融英語の上達を目指す学生や社会人の方々を対象とした英文集であり、特に金融・経済の話題について英語で表現する力を身につけたいと願う方々に適しています。

　本書の特徴は、次のとおりです。

① 英字新聞・英文雑誌や書籍で頻繁に用いられるキーワード700個を選び、テーマ別に分類。

② 各キーワードを含むセンテンスを書籍・新聞・雑誌・論文等から引用（適宜書き換えた箇所があります）。

③ 700のセンテンスは、内容と構文・語句の両方の観点から厳選。

④ 学習しやすいよう、英文と日本語訳を左右見開きに掲載。

　700のセンテンスは、出典となった書籍等に使われている文をなるべくそのまま使用しているため、部分的にはむずかしい箇所もありますが、大部分は基本的な英語であり、丸ごと暗記するにも適しています。金融英語に限らず、英作文の正攻法は、多くの英文に接し、それらを真似ることから始まります。

　本書を通じて、金融英語を幅広く習得できるとともに、金融・経済の概観がつかめるようになると考えています。内容面と英語表現の両面について網羅性が高く密度の濃い金融英語の入門書が少ない現状において、本書が意欲の高い方々を満足させる１冊になることを願っています。

　最後に、本書を完成させるにあたり、北山文脩氏（元・住友

信託銀行）にすべての章にわたって貴重なご指摘を数多くいただくなど、多大なご協力いただきました。厚く御礼申し上げます。

平成25年3月

砺 波　元

目　次

第 1 章　　経　済

1. 経　済 *Economy* ……………………………………2
2. Ｇ Ｄ Ｐ *Gross Domestic Product* ………4
3. 景　気 *Economic Conditions* ………………8
4. 物　価 *Prices* …………………………………14
5. 国際経済 *International Economy* ……………18
6. 貿　易 *International Trade* ………………24
7. 為　替 *Foreign Exchange* …………………28
8. 通　貨 *Currencies* ……………………………34
9. 家　計 *Household Economy* …………………40
10. 社会保険 *Social Insurance* ……………………48
11. 財　政 *Public Finance* ………………………52
12. 税　金 *Taxes* …………………………………54

第 2 章　　経営・財務

13. 財務諸表 *Financial Statements* ………………62
14. 会　計 *Accounting* …………………………72
15. 財務分析 *Financial Analysis* …………………76
16. コーポレートファイナンス *Corporate Finance* …………82
17. 銀行借入れ *Bank Loan* ……………………………92
18. 信用リスク *Credit Risk* …………………………96

19 証 券 化 *Securitization* ……………………………………100
20 コーポレートガバナンス・雇用
　　Corporate Governance & Employment ……………………104
21 M ＆ A *Mergers and Acquisitions* ……………………108
22 産　　業 *Industries* ………………………………………116

第3章　金　融

23 金融市場 *Financial Markets* …………………………124
24 金融機関 *Financial Institutions* ………………………128
25 金　利 *Interest Rates* …………………………………132
26 金融規制 *Financial Regulation* ………………………136
27 金融政策 *Monetary Policy* ……………………………140
28 証券市場 *Securities Market* …………………………148
29 株　式 *Stocks* …………………………………………152
30 債　券 *Bonds* …………………………………………158
31 デリバティブ *Derivatives* ……………………………168
32 投資信託 *Investment Trusts* …………………………174
33 投資ファンド *Investment Funds* ……………………180
34 証券投資 *Portfolio Investment* ………………………184

引用文献 ………………………………………………………192
索引（英文）…………………………………………………195
索引（和文）…………………………………………………206

第1章 経済

Economy

1 The **Great Depression** of the 1930s was the most severe economic downturn of the twentieth century.

2 On October 19, 1987, known as **Black Monday**, the Dow Jones index of the stock market fell a dramatic 22.6% in one day.

3 The BOJ was exposed to severe criticism that prolonged monetary easing since the latter half of the 1980s had brought about the **bubble economy**.

4 During Japan's so-called "**lost decade**" of the 1990s, the economy managed to grow by about 1.7% per year.

5 The US economy experienced an extraordinary performance in the late 1990s which is referred to as the "**new economy**".

6 **Asian financial crisis** began in Thailand in July 1997 when the value of the Thai currency plummeted following the country's abandonment of its pegged exchange system.

7 The well-known **dot.com bubble** between 1995 and 2000 was characterized by rapid growth in the value of Internet stocks.

1 経　済

1　1930年代の世界大恐慌は、20世紀で最も厳しい景気悪化であった。

2　ブラックマンデーとして知られる1987年10月19日に、ダウジョーンズ平均株価は1日で22.6%暴落した。

3　日本銀行は、1980年代後半以後の長期にわたる金融緩和がバブル経済を引き起こしたという厳しい批判を浴びた。

4　日本における1990年代のいわゆる「失われた10年」の間、日本国経済は年率1.7%ほどの成長をどうにか維持してきた。

5　米国経済は、1990年代末期に「ニューエコノミー」と呼ばれる目覚しい景気拡張を経験した。

6　アジア通貨危機は、1997年7月にタイを震源に生じた。タイでは固定相場制の放棄を契機に通貨価値が急落したのである。

7　1995年から2000年に生じた、かの有名なITバブルは、インターネット関連株における急成長により特徴づけられた。

8 Between 2002 and 2003, the U.S. economy had a **jobless recovery** as gains in productivity drastically outpaced increases in employment.

9 The **subprime mortgage crisis** in the United States resulted from the granting of mortgages to borrowers with weak credit quality.

10 In September 2008, the subprime mortgage crisis that began earlier in 2007 evolved into a global **financial crisis**.

11 The **European debt crisis** started as a small local policy shock in Greece.

2 Gross Domestic Product

12 In 2010, China's **gross domestic product** exceeded that of Japan to become the second largest in the world.

13 In 1989, Japan ranked fourth in the world in terms of **per capita GDP**; by 2010, its rank had plummeted to 24th.

14 The **nominal GDP** in Japan has remained at a level close to 500 trillion yen over the past decade.

8 2002年から2003年にかけて、米国経済では、生産性の伸びが雇用の増加を大きくしのぐことで、**雇用なき景気回復**がみられた。

9 米国における**サブプライム住宅ローン危機**は、信用度の低い借り手への住宅ローン貸付が原因となり生じた。

10 2007年の初めに生じたサブプライム住宅ローン危機は、2008年9月に世界的な**金融危機**へと発展した。

11 **欧州債務危機**は、ギリシャという小規模な地域の財政ショックから始まった。

2 GDP

12 2010年に、中国の**国内総生産**は日本を上回り、世界第2位の規模となった。

13 1989年、日本は**1人当りGDP**で世界第4位となったが、2010年までに24位へと急落した。

14 日本の**名目GDP**は、過去10年にわたり500兆円付近で推移してきた。

15 The greater the difference between nominal GDP growth and **real GDP** growth, the greater the rate of inflation.

16 **Consumer spending** accounts for nearly 60% of Japan's GDP.

17 **Investment spending**, including business investment and investment in new homes, is sensitive to interest rates.

18 A short-term increase in **government spending** can provide a stabilizing boost to the economy, but in general it diverts resources from productive growth.

19 **Residential investment** tends to weaken as the rise in long-term interest rates progresses.

20 **Business investment** decisions are influenced by the expected profit rate and the real interest rate.

21 Unplanned **inventory investment** is the accumulation of unsold stock or raw materials due to unanticipated fluctuations in demand.

22 Developing countries have the capacity for faster **GDP growth** than more mature industrial economies.

23 In general, when the **output gap** is positive, the inflation rate tends to rise.

15 名目GDP成長率と**実質GDP**成長率との差が大きいほど、インフレ率が高い。

16 **消費支出**が、日本のGDPの60%近くを占めている。

17 設備投資と住宅投資を含む**投資支出**は、金利に敏感に反応する。

18 短期的な**政府支出**の増加は景気の安定化を後押ししうるが、通常はそれにより資源が生産的な成長に回らなくなる。

19 長期金利の上昇が進むにつれて、**住宅投資**は弱まる傾向にある。

▶ residential investment=housing investment

20 **設備投資**の決定には、予想利益率や実質金利が影響する。

▶ business investment=capital investment

21 意図せざる**在庫投資**は、予期せぬ需要変動による売れ残り在庫もしくは原材料の積増しを意味する。

22 開発途上国は、より成熟した先進工業国の経済に比べ、急速な**GDP成長**をもたらす力をもっている。

23 通常、**需給ギャップ**が正である場合、インフレ率は上昇傾向になる。

▶ 需給ギャップ：経済の供給力と実際の需要との差

24 After the drastic appreciation of the yen, Japan switched from its conventional export-led economic growth to a **domestic-demand**-oriented expansion.

25 For most of the 1980s, Japan had a very favorable balance of payments as a result of high **foreign demand** for its automobiles, electronic products, and other goods.

3 Economic Conditions

26 The factors mainly accounting for the rapid **economic growth** of Japan and Germany are the scientific and technological advancement of these countries.

27 The Japanese economy made a remarkable change from high growth to low but **stable growth** after the mid-1970s.

28 A worldwide **economic recovery** began to take shape in March 2003, soon after the Iraq war began.

29 In October 2007, Japan's longest post-war period of **economic expansion** ended after 69 months.

30 The Japanese economy experienced an unusually sharp **economic slowdown** in the 1990s, which led to a sustained period of deflation.

24 大幅な円高の後、日本は従来の輸出主導型の経済成長から内需拡大路線へと切り替えた。

25 1980年代の大半において、日本の国際収支は、自動車、電気製品、その他製品への強い外需のもと、非常に良好であった。

3　景　気

26 日本とドイツの急速な経済成長の主な要因は、これらの国における科学および技術の進歩である。

27 日本経済は、1970年代中頃より、それまでの高度成長から低成長ではあるけれども安定成長へと著しい変化を遂げた。

28 イラク戦争開始直後の2003年3月に、世界的な景気回復に目鼻がつき始めた。

29 2007年10月に、日本の戦後最長の景気拡大期間は69カ月をもって終了した。

30 日本経済は、1990年代にまれにみる急速な景気失速を経験し、それにより持続的なデフレ期がもたらされた。

31 The subprime mortgage crisis triggered a global financial crisis followed by a global **recession**.

32 The most dangerous type of **depression** is caused by the bursting of an investment bubble.

33 Japan suffered through a long and painful **stagnation** that began in 1989 and continued through 2005.

34 Generally, the **business cycle** consists of four states: the peak, recession, the trough, and recovery.

35 **Economic indicators** fall into three broad categories: leading indicators, coincident indicators, and lagging indicators.

36 In the Bank of Japan's Tankan Survey, the **diffusion index** rose from zero at the end of 2003 to 16 in the first quarter of 2006.

37 The University of Michigan's **consumer confidence index** is a leading indicator of the consumer's willingness to spend.

38 **Industrial production**, aside from being directly affected by GDP growth, is also positively related to investment.

39 Actual **machinery orders** act as a leading index for equipment investments some six months ahead.

31 サブプライム住宅ローン危機は世界的な金融危機、ひいては世界的な景気後退への引き金となった。

▸ recession=economic downturn

32 最も危険な不況は、投資バブルの崩壊により引き起こされるタイプである。

33 日本は、1989年に始まり2005年まで続く、長く、厳しい景気停滞を耐え忍んだ。

34 通常、景気循環は好況、後退、不況、回復の４局面からなる。

35 経済指標は、先行、一致、遅行の３指標に大きく分類される。

36 日本銀行の短観では、景気動向指数は2003年度の終わりのゼロから、2006年度の第１四半期にはプラス16まで改善した。

37 ミシガン大学消費者信頼感指数は、消費者マインド（消費意欲）に関する先行指標である。

38 鉱工業生産は、GDP成長による直接の影響を受けるほか、投資とも正の相関関係にある。

39 実質機械受注は、設備投資より６カ月ほど先行する指標として作用する。

40 A **housing start** implies a given level of demand for construction materials and labor over the next few months and a housing completion at the end of that period.

41 In most countries, **housing permits** are a useful leading indicator for housing investment.

42 The retail sector places considerable emphasis on **like-for-like sales** growth as an indicator of performance.

43 The **unemployment rate** in Japan peaked in FY2002 at 5.4%.

44 Analysts generally believe the economy is adding jobs when **jobless claims** are consistently below 400,000.

45 **Nonfarm payroll** employment is often considered a better indicator of current economic conditions than household employment.

46 The original **Phillips curve** suggests an inverse relationship between wage inflation and unemployment.

40 住宅着工件数は、向こう数カ月間における一定レベルの建設資材および労働需要、ならびに当該期間終了時における住宅完成件数を意味する。

41 多くの国々において、住宅着工許可件数は住宅投資の有効な先行指数である。

42 小売業では、業績評価指標として既存店ベースの売上高の伸び率にかなりの重点を置く。

43 日本の失業率は2002年度に5.4%のピークに達した。

44 アナリストは、一般的に、失業保険申請件数（米国）が一貫して40万人を下回るかどうかが雇用増の目安になると考える。

45 非農業部門雇用者数（米国）は、家計調査の雇用者数よりも現在の経済状況をよく示す指標であるとみなされることが多い。

46 オリジナルのフィリップス曲線は、賃金上昇率と失業率との負の関係を示している。

4 Prices

47 The **consumer price index** is the primary inflation measure for the BOJ, even though it does not have an inflation target.

48 The main purpose of **corporate goods price index** is to investigate price movements that reflect most sensitively the supply and demand conditions of individual goods.

49 **Producer price indices** shed light on cost pressures affecting domestic production and are more useful than wholesale price indices.

50 The **GDP deflator** covers only goods and services produced domestically, whereas the CPI includes all goods and services purchased by consumers.

51 The BOJ pursues **price stability** as its primary goal ideally to maintain an economic environment in which there is neither inflation nor deflation.

52 When **inflation** finally peaked in 1980, consumer prices around the world rose by nearly 18% over the year before.

53 The **inflation rate** in the world as a whole remained in two digits in almost all years during 1973-1995.

4　物　価

47 **消費者物価指数**は、たとえインフレターゲットが設定されないにしても、日本銀行にとって主要なインフレ判断基準である。

48 **企業物価指数**の主な目的は、各商品の需給動向を最も敏感に反映する価格動向を調査することにある。

49 **生産者物価指数**では、国内生産に影響を及ぼすコスト上昇圧力が明らかとなり、卸売物価指数よりも有用である。

50 消費者物価指数が消費者の購入する財・サービスすべてを含むのに対して、**GDPデフレーター**は国内で生産される財・サービスのみ取り扱う。

▶ GDPデフレーター：実質GDPを計算する際の物価指数（名目GDP ÷ 実質GDP）

51 日本銀行は、インフレでもデフレでもない経済環境を理想的に維持するために、主要目標として**物価安定**を追求する。

52 1980年に**インフレ**がついに頂点に達した時、世界中で消費者物価が上昇し、前年よりほぼ18％増となった。

53 世界全体の**インフレ率**は、1973年から1995年までの期間のほとんどすべての年で2桁を維持した。

54 It is generally believed that the upward pressure on oil prices during the 1970s has been an important factor causing **cost inflation** and unemployment.

55 Although Japan continued to be world's largest creditor nation, **asset value inflation** collapsed after reaching a peak at the end of the 1980s.

56 Fiscal policy, a traditional source of **inflation pressure**, is also identified as an important determinant of inflation.

57 Real estate as an asset class has traditionally been regarded as a **hedge against inflation**.

58 A number of countries have used **inflation targeting** to bring their inflation rates down.

59 **Stagflation**, which is the combination of high unemployment and high inflation, hit the US economy with full force in 1974.

60 In 1989, Argentina suffered from **hyperinflation** that reached 5000% annually, which, at the time, was the highest rate in the world.

61 Japan experienced **disinflation** in the first half of the 1990s and deflation from 1994 through 2004.

54 1970年代における石油価格の上昇圧力が、コストインフレと失業を引き起こす重要な要因となってきたというのが定説だ。

▶ コストインフレ：賃金や原材料費の急激な上昇により引き起こされるインフレ

55 日本は世界最大の債権国であり続けたが、資産インフレは1980年代の終わりにピークに達した後、崩壊した。

56 従来のインフレ圧力源である財政政策は、インフレの重要な決定因子であるともされている。

▶ インフレ圧力：インフレを引き起こす要因がインフレになる方向に推移していること

57 アセットクラス（資産の種類）としての不動産は、昔からインフレヘッジとみなされてきた。

58 多くの国で、インフレ率の引下げ目的でインフレ目標政策が導入されてきた。

▶ インフレ目標政策：中央銀行が物価上昇率の数値目標を定める金融政策

59 高い失業率と高いインフレ率が共存するスタグフレーションによって、1974年に米国経済は大打撃を受けた。

▶ スタグフレーション：景気停滞下のインフレ

60 1989年、アルゼンチンは年率5000％に達するハイパーインフレに見舞われた。それは当時では世界最高のインフレ率であった。

61 日本は1990年代前半にディスインフレを、1994年から2004年までデフレを経験した。

▶ ディスインフレ：インフレからは脱したがデフレにはなっていない状態

62 Overly restrictive monetary policy in the early 1990s was a major cause of Japan's **deflation**.

63 Japan's economy was once on the brink of a **deflationary spiral**, as nominal GDP began to decrease amid the credit crunch in 1998.

64 A **commodity price** index is preferable as a leading indicator of inflation.

65 In July 2008, the **crude oil price** peaked at $144 a barrel.

66 **Gold prices** usually respond positively to the expectation of increased inflation.

67 In the inflation-dominated 1970s, **real assets** such as real estate, gold, and antiques were highly regarded as hedges against declining purchasing power.

5 International Economy

68 The international **balance of payments** is divided into two major accounts. They are the current account and the capital and financial account.

69 Japan has had a **current account** surplus fluctuating around 2% of GDP.

70 The **balance of trade** is the dominant part of the current account balance.

62 1990年代初めにおける過度な金融引締政策が、日本のデフレの主な原因であった。

63 日本経済はかつてデフレスパイラルの危機に瀕していた。ちょうど1998年、金融収縮のただなかで、名目GDPが減少し始めた時である。

▶ デフレスパイラル：物価の下落と経済活動の低迷が繰り返される状況

64 商品価格指数はインフレの先行指標として好ましい。

65 2008年7月、原油価格は1バレル当り144ドルというピークに至った。

66 金価格は通常、インフレ増進の予想にプラスに反応する。

67 インフレが優勢であった1970年代には、不動産、金、骨董品などの実物資産が、下降する購買力に対する防御手段として高く評価されていた。

5　国際経済

68 国際収支は、経常収支と資本収支の主に2つの勘定項目に分けられる。

69 日本の経常収支の黒字額は、対GDP比2％前後で変動してきた。

▶ 経常収支：国際収支のうち経常取引に関するもの（貿易収支、サービス収支、所得収支、経常移転収支の総称）

70 貿易収支は、経常収支の主要な部門である。

71 The deficit in the U.S. current account in recent years has usually been offset by a **financial account** surplus.

72 The **capital account** is composed of all the transfers of financial assets and the acquisition of nonproduced and nonfinancial assets.

73 Japan increased direct foreign investment and became the world's largest **creditor nation**.

74 The United States is now the world's number one **debtor nation**, in both gross and net terms.

75 Japan has had very little **external debt**; consequently, a precipitous fall in the value of the yen would not create a foreign payments crisis.

76 Traditionally, **foreign currency reserves** were judged adequate when they were equal in value to three months' worth of imports.

77 Japan's outward **direct investment** vastly exceeds its inward direct investment.

78 The early 1990s were characterized by a surge of **capital inflows** to developing countries.

79 When a currency crisis occurs, investors quickly lose confidence in the currency, which leads to a large-scale **capital outflow** and a further currency depreciation.

71 近年における米国の経常収支赤字は、大概、**投資収支**の黒字分で相殺されてきた。
▶ 投資収支：居住者と非居住者との間の金融資産負債の取引

72 **その他資本収支**は、あらゆる金融資産の取引や非生産・非金融資産の取得にて構成される。
▶ その他資本収支：資本収支（居住者と非居住者との間の取引）のうち投資収支以外の収支

73 日本は対外直接投資をふやし、世界最大の**債権国**となった。

74 米国はいまやグロス・ネット両観点からして、世界最大の**債務国**である。

75 日本はほとんど**対外債務**を保有してこなかったため、結果的に円の急落が起きても対外支払危機は生じないであろう。

76 慣例上、**外貨準備高**は、輸入総額の3カ月分に相当する保有高をもってして適正水準であると判断されていた。

77 日本からの対外**直接投資**は、日本への対内直接投資をおおいに上回っている。
▶ 直接投資：海外の企業に対して、経営を支配することを目的に行われる投資

78 1990年代初頭の特徴としては、開発途上国への**資本流入**が急増した点があげられる。

79 通貨危機が生じると、投資家によるその通貨への信頼が瞬く間に失われ、それが大規模な**資本流出**とさらなる通貨の下落をまねく。

80 When financial crisis erupted in Southeast Asia, the **International Monetary Fund** provided some US$36 billion in financial support.

81 In 2009, the IMF injected $250 billion into the global economy through a new allocation of **Special Drawing Rights**.

82 In contrast to the IMF, The **World Bank** has always specialized in relatively long-term loans used to fund long-term development and growth.

83 **Emerging markets** have been the main drivers of growth in the world economy.

84 More than 40% of the expansion in the world economy between 2003 and 2007 was due to the growth of the **BRICs**.

85 **Islamic finance** is a rapidly expanding market and is one of the fastest growing areas of international finance.

86 After the increase in the price of oil stimulated by the OPEC in the mid-1970s, large amounts of what have been called **petrodollars** flooded international money market.

80 東南アジアで金融危機が勃発した際、IMF（国際通貨基金）は360億米ドルもの財政支援を行った。

81 2009年、IMFはSDR（特別引出し権）の新規割当てにより、世界経済に2,500億米ドルを注入した。

▶ SDR（特別引出し権）：IMFに加盟する国がもつ資金引出し権

82 IMFとは対照的に、世界銀行は常に長期的な発展と成長に対する比較的長期的な貸付に専念してきた。

83 新興市場は、世界経済の成長の主要な牽引力となっている。

84 2003年から2007年にかけての世界経済拡大の40％以上は、BRICs（ブリックス）の成長によるものであった。

▶ BRICs：高度経済成長が見込まれる4カ国（ブラジル・ロシア・インド・中国）の総称

85 イスラム金融市場は急速に拡大しており、国際金融のなかで最も速い成長をみせている地域の1つである。

86 1970年代半ばにOPECによる攻勢を受け石油価格が上昇すると、オイルダラーと呼ばれる大量の資金が国際金融市場にあふれた。

6 International Trade

87 Government restrictions on **foreign trade** are usually aimed at protecting domestic producers from foreign competition.

88 Global **trade volume** has accelerated sharply since the end of the Cold War.

89 In 2007, China became Japan's largest **trading partner** and counted 17.7% of Japan's total trade.

90 Japan's **export dependence** in terms of the GDP ratio is sharply lower than the average of about 30% in the whole trading world.

91 Japan's **import dependence** for energy requirements is remarkably high.

92 China has maintained a large **trade surplus** in recent years, adding to its large foreign exchange reserves.

93 Japan posted a **trade deficit** in 2011 for the first time in 31 years.

94 **Trade barriers** have been removed in many countries, through participation in regional agreements and broader international arrangements.

95 The complexity of Japan's distribution system is often criticized as a **non-tariff barrier**.

6 貿 易

87 政府による貿易規制は、大概、国際競争から国内生産者を保護することを目的としている。

88 世界の貿易量は、冷戦終結後に急伸してきた。

89 2007年、中国は日本の最大の貿易相手国となり、日本の貿易総額の17.7%を占めた。

90 日本の対GDP比の輸出依存度は、世界貿易全体における平均30%ほどと比べて著しく低い。

91 エネルギー需要に対する日本の輸入依存度は、著しく高い。

92 近年、中国は多額の貿易黒字を維持し、豊富な外貨準備高を増額している。

93 日本は2011年に31年ぶりの貿易赤字を計上した。

94 地域協定やより広域な国際協定への参加を通して、多くの国々において貿易障壁が取り除かれてきた。

95 日本の流通システムの複雑性は、しばしば非関税障壁であるとの批判を受けている。

96 The US-China **trade imbalance** has become a source of trade friction between the two countries.

97 China's huge trade surplus with the United States has shifted the focus of **trade friction** from between the United States and Japan to between the United States and China.

98 The share of **capital goods** in Japan's total export items has been rising consistently since the high-growth period.

99 **Consumer goods** productions have been increasingly replaced by imports, reflecting a shift to overseas production of home electric appliances, etc.

100 The Netherlands is considered an extremely **open economy** because it imports and exports about two thirds of its GDP.

101 Although few countries practice **free trade**, most economists continue to hold up free trade as a desirable policy.

102 The **World Trade Organization** was established in 1995 to replace GATT as the international framework for international trade negotiations.

96 米中間の貿易不均衡は、両国間における貿易摩擦の原因となってきた。

97 中国の巨額な対米貿易黒字によって、日米間の貿易摩擦の焦点が米中間へとシフトした。

98 日本の総輸出品目における資本財の占める割合は、高度成長期以後、着実に増加してきている。

▶ 資本財：ある財を生み出すために投入される機械・設備・原料などの財

99 家電等の海外生産へのシフトを反映して、消費財の生産は、ますます輸入品に置き換えられつつある。

▶ 消費財：個人や家庭で使用するために購入する製品

100 オランダは極度な開放経済国家だと考えられているが、それはGDPの約3分の2を輸出入が占めているからである。

▶ 開放経済：外国と金融や貿易の取引をしている経済

101 自由貿易を実行する国はほとんどないが、望ましい政策として自由貿易を支持し続ける経済学者が多い。

102 世界貿易機関（WTO）は、1995年、国際的な貿易交渉の世界的な枠組みとして、GATT（関税貿易一般協定）にかわり設立された。

7 Foreign Exchange

103 Anyone who makes a profit in the **foreign exchange market** is matched by someone else making a loss. It is a zero sum game.

104 The **exchange rate** is determined by the forces of demand and supply of the foreign currency in the market.

105 The **real exchange rate** is a measure of change in the relative purchasing power of the two currencies concerned.

106 A real **effective exchange rate** will give a measure of the overall competitiveness of domestic goods on world markets.

107 The United Kingdom and the United States account for half of total world **foreign exchange trading**.

108 For foreign financial assets such as stocks and bonds, hedging against **foreign exchange risk** substantially reduces the risk of international portfolios.

109 **Foreign exchange hedging** may decrease the gains from international diversification.

7　為　替

103 **外国為替市場**において利益をあげる人がいれば、それに匹敵する損失を出している人がいる。ゼロサムゲームである。

104 **為替レート**は市場におけるその外貨への需給要因で決まる。

105 **実質為替レート**は、当該2通貨間の相対的な購買力からみた交換尺度である。

▶ 実質為替レート：2国間の物価の違いを調整した為替レート

106 実質**実効為替レート**によって、自国製品の世界市場における総合的な競争力を測ることができる。

▶ 実効為替レート：1国の通貨の他通貨に対する相対的価値を示す指標

107 英国と米国とで、世界の全**外国為替取引**の半数を占めている。

108 株式や債券などの海外金融資産に対して、**為替リスク**へのヘッジは国際ポートフォリオのリスクを大幅に軽減する。

109 **為替ヘッジ**は、国際分散投資による利益を減らす可能性がある。

110 Multinational corporations need **exchange rate forecasts** to make decisions on hedging payables and receivables, short-term financing and investment, capital budgeting, and long-term financing.

111 Most central banks conduct foreign exchange interventions in the **spot market**.

112 Part of the global excess liquidity can be explained by the global **carry trade**.

113 Many economists believe that **purchasing power parity** describes the forces that determine exchange rates in the long run.

114 The **international monetary system** has evolved over the years from the gold standard to what is now known as the floating exchange rate system.

115 As the depression progressed, country after country departed from the **gold standard**.

116 The **Bretton Woods System** ended when dollar-gold convertibility was terminated in 1971.

117 Under a **fixed exchange rate system**, governments must sometimes intervene in the foreign exchange market to maintain the exchange rate.

118 Through the period of the **floating exchange rate system**, the yen appreciated sharply against the dollar.

110 多国籍企業は、債務・債権のヘッジングや短期の出融資、資本予算策定、長期融資につき意思決定するために、**為替見通し**を必要とする。

111 ほとんどの中央銀行は**直物市場**において外国為替介入を行う。

112 世界的な過剰流動性は、部分的にはグローバルな**キャリートレード**によるものといえる。

▶ キャリートレード：金利の低い通貨で資金を借りて金利の高い通貨に投資することで利益を得る手法

113 **購買力平価**が長期的な為替レートを決定する要因であるとする説を支持する経済学者が多い。

▶ 購買力平価：為替レートは自国通貨と外国通貨の購買力の比率によって決定されるという説

114 **国際通貨制度**は、金本位制から変動為替相場制として現在知られる制度に至るまで、長い年月をかけて発展を遂げてきた。

115 不況が深刻化するにつれ、各国が次々と**金本位制**から離脱した。

116 **ブレトンウッズ体制**は、1971年における米ドルの金兌換停止をもって終結した。

117 **固定為替相場制**のもとでは、政府は時に外国為替市場に介入し、為替レートを維持する必要がある。

118 **変動為替相場制**へ切り替えられてから、円は米ドルに対して急激に値上りした。

119 The **Plaza Accord** aimed at adjusting the overvalued exchange rate of the US dollar.

120 The Bank of Japan alone spent ¥35 trillion on foreign **exchange intervention** in a 15-month period during 2003 and early 2004.

121 In 1985, the G-5 central banks agreed to stop the rise of the US dollar through **coordinated intervention**.

122 Most central banks use **sterilized intervention** to neutralize the expansionary effects on the money supply.

123 **Unsterilized intervention** has long been recognized to have a greater effect on exchange rates than sterilized, because it directly affects domestic money supply.

124 The rapid **appreciation of the yen** accelerated as a result of the Plaza Accord in September 1985.

125 The large twin deficits in the United States could lead to a rapid **depreciation of the dollar**.

126 If exports and imports adjust gradually to real exchange rate changes, the current account may follow a **J-curve** pattern after a real currency depreciation.

119 プラザ合意の目的は、過度に高い米ドルの為替レートを調整することであった。

120 日本銀行は、2003年から2004年初期にわたる15カ月間に、単独で35兆円の為替介入を行った。

121 1985年に、G5（先進5カ国）の中央銀行は協調介入を通じて米ドルの高騰に歯止めを掛けることで合意した。

122 多くの中央銀行が、貨幣供給への景気刺激効果を相殺する目的で不胎化介入を行う。

▶ 不胎化介入：為替介入と同時に金融調節を行って中央銀行通貨の増減を相殺すること

123 自国の通貨供給量に直接影響を及ぼすがゆえに、非不胎化介入のほうが不胎化よりも為替レートに及ぼす効果が大きいと長年考えられてきた。

124 1985年9月のプラザ合意を受けて、急激な円高が加速した。

125 米国の巨額の双子の赤字によって、急激なドル安が引き起こされた。

126 輸出および輸入が実質為替レートの変動に徐々に順応する場合には、経常収支は実質的な通貨下落後にJカーブのパターンをとる可能性がある。

▶ Jカーブ：為替レートの上昇が短期的には貿易収支を赤字化させるが、長期的には貿易収支を黒字化させる現象

8 Currencies

127 **Currency trading** in foreign exchange markets amounts to more than ten times the value of imported and exported goods.

128 Differential inflation rates between countries are a prime cause of **currency fluctuations**.

129 Under the fixed exchange rate system, countries with a negative balance of trade often try to reduce their economic problems by **currency devaluation**.

130 The **foreign currency** will appreciate when the home country's inflation exceeds the foreign country's inflation.

131 The 1920s and 1930s were a time of transition as the **key currency** shifted from the pound sterling to the US dollar.

132 Swiss franc continues to be regarded as a **safe-haven currency** in times of uncertainty or currency crisis.

133 A **dollar peg** ensures stability of income flows from abroad and stabilizes fluctuations in financial wealth.

134 The growth in **offshore currency trading** has gone hand in hand with that of offshore banking.

8　通　貨

127　外国為替市場における通貨取引高は、輸出入品の価値にして、その10倍を超える金額である。

128　各国間のインフレ率の差が、通貨変動を引き起こす１つの主な原因である。

129　固定為替相場制では、貿易赤字国は通貨切下げにより自国の経済問題を軽減しようとするケースが多い。

130　自国のインフレが外国のインフレを上回るとき、外貨は値上りする。

131　1920年代および1930年代は、基軸通貨が英ポンドから米ドルへと切り替わった変遷の時代であった。

▶ 基軸通貨：世界的に流通し、国際間の決済や金融取引において中核的機能を果たす通貨

132　スイスフランは、不確実性や通貨危機の時代において、避難通貨とみなされ続けている。

▶ 避難通貨：世界のどこかで危機や事件が起きたときに一時的に買われる通貨

133　ドルペッグ制は自国への安定的な海外資本流入を確保するとともに、金融資産の騰落を安定化させる。

▶ ドルペッグ制：自国通貨の為替レートを米ドルと連動させる制度

134　オフショア通貨取引はオフショア金融の成長とともに発展してきた。

135 One of the major causes of a **currency crisis** is the disequilibrium of the exchange rate from its market-determined rate.

136 Having experienced the Asian financial crisis, the thirteen East and Southeast Asian countries agreed in 2000 to establish a **currency swap arrangement**.

137 The **Japanese yen** has the lowest interest rate of all industrialized countries, so it is the primary currency sold in carry trade.

138 In July 2005, China announced a 2.1% revaluation of the **renminbi**-US dollar exchange rate.

139 The **Hong Kong dollar** is pegged to the US dollar at 7.8 dollars to 1 US$.

140 The once-robust relationship between the **South African rand** and gold has largely dwindled as a result of South Africa's plummeting gold production.

141 The **US dollar** is the currency used most often in international transactions and constitutes more than half of the countries' official reserves.

142 The **Canadian dollar** is what is called a commodity currency.

135 通貨危機の主な原因の１つは、為替レートの市場レートとの不均衡である。

136 アジア通貨危機を経験することで、2000年に東アジア・東南アジアの13の国々が通貨スワップ協定を制定することに合意した。

> ▶通貨スワップ協定：自国の通貨危機の際に自国通貨と引き換えに相手国の通貨を融通してもらう取決め

137 日本円は先進国中で一番金利が低いため、キャリートレードにおいて最も売られている通貨である。

138 2005年７月、中国は人民元の対ドル為替レートの2.1％切上げを発表した。

139 香港ドルは、１米ドル＝7.8香港ドルで米ドルに固定されている。

140 南アフリカランドと金とのかつての確固たる結びつきは、南アフリカの金生産の急激な落込みを受けて大きく希薄化した。

141 米ドルは国際取引において最も頻繁に使用される通貨であり、各国の公式外貨準備の半数以上を占めている。

142 カナダドルはいわゆる資源国通貨である。

143 For the **Australian dollar**, a relatively high-interest-rate currency, tail events are more common for depreciations than for appreciations.

144 After Brazil's exchange rate crisis in 1999, the **Brazilian real** depreciated sharply and started floating.

145 In mid-August 1998, the **Russian ruble** was devalued to about one-third of its value versus the dollar.

146 Because the United Kingdom is an oil producer, the **UK pound sterling** can be affected more directly by oil prices than other currencies.

147 Since 1995, the **Swiss franc** and the Japanese yen have been low-rate currencies used worldwide for the carry trade.

148 On 1st January 1999, the **euro** was introduced as the single currency of eleven EU Member States.

149 The adoption of the euro as a **single currency** has made the EU a major international monetary power.

150 In 1979, the European Union announced the formation of the **European Monetary System** as part of its aim toward greater monetary integration among its members.

143 比較的に高利回りの通貨である豪ドルについていえば、テールイベント（想定外の突発的な事象）は切上げよりも切下げに対してよくみられる。

144 1999年のブラジル通貨危機の後、ブラジルレアルは大幅に切り下げられ、変動相場制が始まった。

145 1998年8月半ば、ロシアルーブルは米ドルに対しその価値を3分の1にまで切り下げられた。

146 英国は産油国であるため、英ポンドは他の通貨と比べ石油価格により直接影響を受ける可能性がある。

147 1995年以降、スイスフランと日本円はキャリートレードにおいて金利の低い通貨として世界中で使用されてきた。

148 1999年1月1日、ユーロは、EU加盟国11カ国の統一通貨として導入された。

149 統一通貨としてのユーロの導入によって、EUは国際金融において大きな力をもつ存在となった。

150 1979年、欧州連合は加盟国内におけるより強固な金融統合を目指す一環として、欧州通貨制度（EMS）を設立すると発表した。

151 At the beginning of 1999, the European Monetary System became the **European Monetary Union** with the introduction of the euro.

152 The **Stability and Growth Pact** required member countries to aim at budget deficits smaller than 3% of GDP.

153 More than half of **Eurocurrency** deposits are in negotiable certificates of deposit with maturities of at least 30 days.

154 The **Eurodollar** market developed after World War II as a market for dollar-denominated deposits and loans.

155 Much of current international banking business is conducted in relatively unregulated banking centers known as **Euromarkets**.

9 Household Economy

156 Generally, **national income** of a country is regarded as an index of welfare.

157 There is a high correlation between growth in real private consumption expenditure and real personal **disposable income**.

151 1999年の初めに、欧州通貨制度（EMS）は、ユーロの導入と同時に欧州経済通貨同盟（EMU）となった。

152 安定成長協定では、各加盟国は財政赤字を対GDP比3％以下に抑える必要があるとした。

▶ 安定成長協定：EMUを促進・維持していくための財政政策の運営に関する合意

153 ユーロカレンシー預金の半数以上は、最低30日間の払戻期限（満期日）の定めのある譲渡性預金である。

▶ ユーロカレンシー：その通貨の母国以外の市場において取引される通貨

154 ユーロダラー市場は、ドル建て預金および貸付に対する市場として第二次世界大戦後に発展を遂げた。

▶ ユーロダラー：米国以外の市場において取引される米ドル通貨（ユーロカレンシーの一種）

155 現在の国際的な銀行業務の多くは、ユーロ市場として知られる比較的規制の緩やかな取引市場にてとり行われている。

▶ ユーロ市場：通貨の発行国以外でのその通貨の取引市場

9　家　計

156 通常、1国の国民所得は富の指標とみなされる。

157 実質個人消費支出と実質可処分所得との間には、高い相関関係がみられる。

▶ 可処分所得：家計の収入から非消費支出を差し引いたもので、個人が自由に使える所得

158 The rising level of **income inequality** is explained in part by the increasing share of temporary workers.

159 The **financial assets** held by Japanese households amount to around 1,500 trillion yen.

160 Most financial planners suggest having at least six months' worth of **living expenses** in cash.

161 Japan's **medical expenses** relative to GDP are at a low level.

162 Many economists believe that the high Japanese **saving rate** is a key to the rapid growth Japan experienced in the decades after World War II.

163 Generally speaking, the higher the interest rates on **savings accounts**, the greater the proportion of income that families will put into savings.

164 **Time deposits** pay higher interest than savings accounts, the rate increasing with time.

165 Banks pay **deposit insurance** premiums depending on the riskiness of their assets, as determined by their government supervisors.

166 A bank **pay-off** system limits government protection of bank deposit up to 10 million yen plus interest.

167 Examples of **secured debt** are a mortgage and an auto loan.

158 所得格差の拡大は、一部には臨時雇用者の割合増加の影響もある。

159 日本の世帯の保有する金融資産額は、約1,500兆円に達する。

160 たいていのファイナンシャルプランナーは、少なくとも6カ月分の生活費に相当する金額を現金で保有することを勧める。

161 日本の対 GDP 比での医療費の水準は低い。

162 日本の高い貯蓄率が、第二次世界大戦後の数十年間における日本の急成長の鍵であると考える経済学者が多い。

163 一般的に、普通預金の金利が高ければ高いほど、家計が所得のうち貯蓄に回す割合がふえる。

164 定期預金は、普通預金よりも金利が高く、利率は期間に応じて高まる。

165 銀行は政府の管理機構が定めたとおりに、自行の資産リスクに応じた預金保険料を支払う。

▶ 預金保険：金融機関が破綻した場合に、その金融機関に預けられている預金を保護する保険

166 銀行のペイオフ制度では、政府による銀行預金の保護は、1,000万円までとその利息に限られる。

▶ ペイオフ：金融機関が破綻した場合に、預金者に一定額の保険金が支払われる仕組み

167 有担保債務の例としては、住宅ローンや自動車ローンがある。

168 **Unsecured debt** is borrowing whose repayment is based solely on the full faith and credit of the debtor.

169 **Fixed-rate mortgages** offer the certainty of a level rate of interest over the life of the mortgage.

170 **Adjustable-rate mortgages** often have lower rates of interest than fixed-rate mortgages over the term of the loan to compensate for assuming the risk of fluctuations in interest rates.

171 In Japan, most residential mortgages are **recourse loans**. If you default, the lender can foreclose on and force the sale of the mortgaged property.

172 The lender of a **nonrecourse loan** generally feels confident that the property used as collateral will be adequate security for the loan.

173 The payouts on a **variable annuity** depend on the performance of the underlying assets relative to the assumed interest rate.

174 A **reverse mortgage** provides borrowed funds based on the market value of the house and the age of the borrower.

168 **無担保債務**は、返済が借り手の十分な信頼と信用のみに基づく借入れである。

169 **固定金利住宅ローン**では、金利はローンの全期間にわたり一定となる。

170 **変動金利住宅ローン**では、金利変動リスクをとることに対する埋合せで、固定金利型と比べてしばしばローン期間中の金利が低くなることがある。

171 日本では、たいていの住宅ローンが**リコースローン**である。債務不履行が生じれば、貸し手は抵当物件を差押えのうえ、これを強制的に売りに出すことができる。

> ▶ リコースローン：返済原資が特定の資産に限定されず、保証人や他の返済原資からの返済を追求できる融資形態

172 **ノンリコースローン**の貸し手は、通常は、担保とする財産がその貸付に対し十分適切な安全性をもつことに信頼を寄せている。

> ▶ ノンリコースローン：特定の資産からのキャッシュフローのみを返済原資とし、本来の借り手には返済の責任が遡及しない融資形態

173 **変額年金**の給付額は、原資の予定利率と比較した運用実績次第で決まる。

174 **リバースモーゲージ**では、借り手の保有住宅の市場価値や年齢に基づき融資される。

> ▶ リバースモーゲージ：自宅を担保に融資を受け、死亡時に自宅を売却して元利合計を一括返済する仕組み

175 **Consumer finance** companies were affected by the introduction of the lower interest rate ceiling under the consumer finance law that was passed at end-2006.

176 Interest on **credit cards** is often offered at a high rate relative to interest on other consumer loans.

177 Unlike credit cards, **debit cards** are not a source of additional funds through borrowing cash because purchase costs are automatically deducted from bank balances.

178 Japan's **real estate** asset amount is estimated to be approximately 2300 trillion yen.

179 At the present time, the real estate establishment of Japan is primarily focused on **commercial property** ownership and loan securitization.

180 **Housing prices** are very high in Japan, primarily because land prices are high.

181 **Land prices** increased three-fold from 1985 to 1990 and declined to the same level by 2000.

175 消費者金融会社は、2006年末に成立した改正貸金業法下での上限金利引下げの導入により打撃を受けた。

176 クレジットカードの利息は、しばしば他の消費者ローンと比べて高い。

177 クレジットカードとは異なり、デビットカードは現金借入れによる追加資金源とはならない。というのも、購入費用は即座に、銀行口座残高から引落しされるためである。

178 日本の不動産の資産額は、約2,300兆円と見積もられている。

179 現在、日本の不動産ビジネスは、主に商業用不動産所有か債権の証券化に集中している。

180 住宅価格は日本では非常に高い。それは主に、地価の高さゆえだ。

181 地価は1985年から1990年にかけて3倍に上昇したが、2000年までに元の水準まで落ち着いた。

10 Social Insurance

182 *Social insurance* programs are financed in large part by contributions from covered employees, employers, or both.

183 Under most Japanese *medical insurance* plans, members are required to pay 10 to 30% of their medical expenses.

184 The Long-Term-Care Insurance System requires all Japanese employees over age 40 to pay premiums for *nursing insurance*.

185 Japan's *employment insurance* is broader than Western unemployment insurance; it includes unemployment benefits and employment promotion.

186 Japan has a pay-as-you-go, defined-benefit, *public pension* system with comprehensive coverage, supplemented by various private pension plans.

187 Japan has a *national pension* insurance system that covers all its citizens, and all adults over the age of 20 are basically obliged to pay contributions.

188 The *Employees' pension* insurance premium is a percentage of standard regular monthly pay and is shared equally by employer and employee.

10 社会保険

182 社会保険制度は、対象となる従業員、事業主またはその両者による保険料を主な財源としている。

183 ほとんどの日本の医療保険制度において、被保険者は掛かった医療費の1～3割を負担する必要がある。

184 介護保険制度により、40歳以上のすべての日本人従業員は介護保険の保険料を支払う必要がある。

▶ nursing insurance=care insurance

185 日本の雇用保険は欧米の失業保険よりも範囲が広く、失業給付と雇用促進を含む。

186 日本には国民皆年金（国民を包括的にカバーする）の賦課方式かつ確定給付型の公的年金制度があり、これを各種私的年金制度が補完している。

187 日本には全国民をカバーする国民年金保険制度があり、原則として20歳以上のすべての成人が保険料を納付する義務を負う。

188 厚生年金保険の保険料は、標準報酬月額（毎月の給与）の一定割合であり、事業主と従業員とで半分ずつ負担する。

189 Widening intergenerational inequality has led to debates regarding 2004 **Pension Reform**.

190 The profitability of **insurance companies** depends in large part on their ability to reduce risks involved in providing insurance.

191 **Life insurance** companies have longer investment time horizons than non-life insurance companies as a result of different expectations of when payments will be required under policies.

192 The main characteristics of a **property and casualty insurance** company's investment portfolio are relatively stable cash flow and good liquidity.

193 **Automobile insurance** is the most important division of the private insurance industry.

194 The **third-sector insurance** market occupies a boundary market between life and non-life insurance markets, such as cancer insurance and medical expense insurance.

195 A **group insurance** plan insures a large number of persons under the terms of a single policy without requiring medical examinations.

196 **Reinsurance** is increasingly important for insurance companies since the need for additional financial capacity is rising.

189 世代間格差の広がりが、2004年の年金制度改革をめぐる議論を巻き起こした。

190 保険会社の収益性は、保険提供にかかわるリスクをいかに軽減できるか、その手腕によるところが大きい。

191 保険の支払発生時期の予測が異なるため、生命保険会社は損害保険会社より投資ホライズン（期間）が長い。

192 損害保険会社の投資ポートフォリオの主な特徴は、比較的安定したキャッシュフローと高い流動性である。

> ▶ property and casualty insurance=general insurance; non-life insurance

193 自動車保険は、民間保険業界において最も重要な分野である。

194 第三分野保険市場は、がん保険や医療保険など、生命保険と損害保険の中間に位置する市場である。

195 団体保険制度は、個々の健康診査なしに、多人数の集団を対象に一括で契約を結ぶ保険である。

196 財務力を上げる必要性が高まっていることから、保険会社にとって再保険の重要性が増している。

11 Public Finance

197 In 1998, the federal government of the United States reached a **budget surplus** for the first time in 30 years.

198 Japan's **budget deficit** in the late 1990s already exceeded 8% of GDP.

199 Many developing nations currently rely on tariffs as a sizable source of **government revenue**.

200 The size of government measured by the ratio of total **government expenditure** to GDP nearly doubled in Japan over the period 1970-2000.

201 To avoid a fall in total expenditures, there is strong political pressure for a **supplementary budget** towards the end of each fiscal year, focused on public works.

202 The Japanese government pledged to achieve a **primary balance** surplus in fiscal 2020.

203 Japan has the highest level of **public debt** among developed countries, standing at almost 200% of GDP.

204 In fiscal 2000, national **debt-servicing costs** surpassed 20 trillion yen for the first time.

205 **Social security expenditure** has been the fastest growing component of public expenditure.

11 財　政

197　1998年、米国連邦政府は30年ぶりの**財政黒字**を達成した。

198　日本の**財政赤字**は1990年代後半に、対 GDP 比ですでに８％を超えた。

199　開発途上国の多くが、現在、**歳入**のかなりの部分を関税に依存している。

200　**歳出**総額の対 GDP 比を尺度とする政府の大きさは、日本では1970年から2000年の間にほぼ倍になった。

201　総支出の減少を回避するため、年度末に向けて公共事業に重点を置く**補正予算**への強い政治的圧力が存在する。

202　日本政府は2020年度に**プライマリーバランス**の黒字化を達成するとの公約を掲げた。

> ▶ プライマリーバランス：国債発行収入を除いた歳入総額と、国債費を除いた歳出総額のバランス

203　日本は**公債**の水準が先進国中で最も高く、対 GDP 比が約200％に達する。

204　2000年度に、**国債費**が初めて20兆円を超えた。

205　**社会保障関係費**は公共支出のなかで最も急速に拡大し続けてきた分野だ。

206 Japan's **military spending** as a proportion of GDP is smaller than that of the other leading powers.

207 The **local government finance** in Japan is almost equivalent in scale to its national general accounts.

208 The most important **fiscal policy** tools used by the government are taxation, government spending, and tax incentives.

209 When government expenditures exceed revenues as a result of deficit spending under a **discretionary fiscal policy**, the deficit is met mainly by issuing public-debt securities.

210 Although still controversial, it looks as if **expansionary fiscal policy** really worked in 2008 and 2009, helping to shorten and moderate the Great Recession.

211 In the 1980s, Japan ran a **contractionary fiscal policy** by reducing budget deficits.

212 The **crowding-out** effect tends to dampen the effects of fiscal policy on aggregate demand.

12　Taxes

213 The **tax system** in Japan, as in other countries, faces increasing pressures from aging and globalization.

206 日本の対 GDP 比での軍事費は、他の主要国と比べて小さい。

207 日本の地方財政の規模は、国の一般会計にほぼ等しい。

208 政府がとる最も重要な財政政策手段は、課税、政府支出、税制優遇策である。

209 裁量的財政政策のもと、赤字財政支出の結果として歳出が歳入を上回ると、赤字分は主に公債発行により埋合せされる。

▶ 裁量的財政政策：景気調節のために政府が実施する財政政策

210 依然として議論は分かれるが、2008年から2009年にかけて積極財政政策は功を奏した模様で、これが大不況を短縮化し和らげるのに役立った。

211 1980年代に、日本は財政赤字を減らすことによる緊縮財政政策をとった。

212 クラウディングアウト効果は、財政政策が総需要に与える効果を鈍らせる傾向にある。

▶ クラウディングアウト：政府支出を行うと利子率が上昇し、民間投資が減少してしまう現象

12 税　金

213 日本の税制にも、他国同様に、高齢化とグローバル化の圧力が押し寄せている。

214 The United States and Japan receive a high percentage of **tax revenue** from income and profits.

215 In recent years, the revenue from **national taxes** has been almost twice that of local taxes.

216 As the main kinds of **local taxes** and their tax rates are regulated by national legislation, the tax burden in Japan is not substantially different from one district to another.

217 It may be said that the tax imposed on income is a **direct tax**, while the tax imposed on expenditure is an indirect tax.

218 One of the features of Japanese tax system often mentioned is that revenues from direct taxes are far greater than those from **indirect taxes**.

219 In common with all the other developed countries, Japan depends upon **individual income tax** for a significant portion of its tax revenues.

220 Japan places greater emphasis on the **corporate income tax**, which is the highest among OECD countries.

221 Japan introduced a **consumption tax** of 3% in 1989 and raised the rate to 5% in 1997.

214 米国と日本は、所得税による税収比率が高い。

215 近年の国税収入は地方税収のほぼ2倍だ。

216 地方税の主な種類や税率については国の法令が定めているため、日本における税負担は地方ごとに大幅に異なることはない。

217 所得課税は直接税、支出に課せられる税は間接税といえるかもしれない。

218 日本の税制の特徴の1つとしてしばしばあげられるのは、直接税からの税収が間接税によるものを大きくしのぐという点だ。

219 他のあらゆる先進諸国と同様に、日本も税収のかなりの部分を個人所得税に依存している。

220 日本は法人税にかなりの重点を置いており、その税率はOECD諸国中で最高水準である。

221 日本は、1989年に3％の消費税を導入し、1997年に税率を5％に引き上げた。

222 **Fixed assets tax** is paid to a municipality by the registered owner of land, buildings, ships or any other depreciable assets.

223 In Japan, land has been used as a device for reducing **inheritance taxes**.

224 The **gift tax** was introduced as a complement to the inheritance tax.

225 The personal income tax system contributes to income redistribution via the **progressive tax rates**.

226 Many countries avoid international **double taxation** by not taxing their taxpayers on foreign source income.

227 Flattening of tax rate schedules has been a major objective of **tax reform** in many countries.

222 固定資産税は土地や建物、船舶、その他償却資産の所有者により自治体へ支払われる税である。

223 日本では、土地は相続税を減らす一手段として用いられてきた。

224 贈与税は相続税を補う目的で導入された。

225 個人所得税制は、累進税率によって所得再分配に貢献する。

▶ 累進税率：課税対象金額が高くなるほど税率が高くなる仕組み

226 多くの国では、国外源泉所得については納税者に課税しないことで、国際的二重課税を回避している。

227 税率表のフラット化が多くの国において税制改革の主要目的であった。

第2章 経営・財務

13 Financial Statements

228 **Financial statements** provide stakeholders with information about the entity's financial position, financial performance, and cash flows.

229 The change in each **balance sheet** item is either a source of funds or a use of funds.

230 The **income statement** is linked to the balance sheet through the retained earnings component of owners' equity.

231 Many readers of the **statement of cash flows** want to know the reasons for the difference between net income and net cash from operating activities.

232 Broadly speaking, **assets** are anything that an organization owns that can be used to generate future revenues.

233 Not all accounting **liabilities** represent legal debt, so in the case of bankruptcy some accounting liabilities would be ignored.

234 **Owner's equity** represents a residual claim to the assets, because the claims of the creditors always come first.

235 Not all **current assets** can be transformed into cash in a short period of time.

13 財務諸表

228 財務諸表は、利害関係者にその組織の財務状況や業績、キャッシュフローにまつわる情報を提供する。

229 貸借対照表の各勘定科目の変化は、資金源もしくは資金の使途を表している。

▶ balance sheet=statement of financial position(財政状態計算書)

230 損益計算書は、純資産(自己資本)のうちの利益剰余金を通じて、貸借対照表と関連し合っている。

▶ income statement=profit and loss statement

231 キャッシュフロー計算書の読み手の多くにとっては、純利益と営業活動による純現金収支との間に生じた差の原因を理解することが目的だ。

232 おおまかにいえば、資産は組織が所有し、将来の収益を生み出すために使用されうるものである。

233 帳簿上のすべての負債が法律上の債務を意味するわけではなく、倒産時には無視される帳簿上の負債もある。

234 自己資本(純資産)は、残余財産分配請求権を意味する。というのも、債権者の権利が常に優先されるからである。

▶ owner's equity=shareholders' equity; net asset; net worth

235 流動資産がすべて短期間に換金されうるとは限らない。

▶ 流動資産:1年以内に現金化・費用化できる資産、または通常の営業活動のなかで発生した資産

236 **Cash equivalents** are held for the purpose of meeting short-term cash commitments rather than for investment or other purposes.

237 **Notes receivable** give the payee a stronger legal claim to assets than accounts receivable.

238 The total of **accounts receivable** written off in an accounting period will rarely equal the estimated uncollectible amount.

239 Materials requirements planning and just-in-time inventory management are two methods for managing demand-dependent **inventories**.

240 **Plant assets**, with the exception of land, should be depreciated over their useful lives to an estimated residual value.

241 **Intangible assets**, which include goodwill, patents, copyrights, trademarks, trade names, and computer software development costs, are usually valued at their cost.

242 The primary reason a company incurs **current liabilities** is to meet its needs for cash during the operating cycle.

243 **Notes payable** give the lender formal proof of the obligation in case legal remedies are needed to collect the debt.

236 現金同等物は、投資目的や他の目的よりも、短期の資金需要を満たす目的で所有される。

237 受取手形は、受取人に対し、売掛金勘定よりも資産に対する強い法的請求権を与える。

238 会計期間中に貸倒れ償却された売掛金の総額が、回収不能見込額と一致することはめったにない。

239 資材所要量計画（MRP）とカンバン方式は、需要依存型の棚卸資産（在庫）管理の２つの手法である。

▶ 棚卸資産（在庫）：会社が販売等の目的で一時的に保有する商品・仕掛品等

240 有形固定資産は、土地を除き、耐用年数にわたって見積残存価額となるまで減価償却されるべきである。

▶ plant asset=tangible fixed asset; property, plant and equipment
▶ 有形固定資産：土地や建物のように実体があり、長期間保有する資産

241 無形固定資産には、営業権、特許権、著作権、商標権、商標商号権、コンピュータソフトウェアの開発費などがあり、通常はその取得原価により評価される。

▶ 無形固定資産：長期にわたり保有する資産のうち目にみえない権利等

242 企業が流動負債を抱える主な理由は、営業循環中における資金需要を満たすためである。

▶ 流動負債：１年以内に返済期日の到来する債務、または通常の営業活動のなかで発生した債務

243 支払手形は、その回収に法的救済が必要な場合に、貸し手にとってその債務の正式な証明となる。

244 When payment terms are extended, the amount in **accounts payable** is expanded to provide an additional source of financing.

245 Examples of **non-current liabilities** are long-term borrowings from financial institutions repayable after twelve months after the balance sheet date.

246 The **capital stock** represents the investment made by the shareholders as a result of purchasing stock.

247 **Additional paid-in capital** represents amounts invested by stockholders in excess of the par value of the common stock.

248 Under most corporate charters, the balance of a corporation's **retained earnings** represents an upper limit on the entity's ability to pay dividends.

249 The effect on a firm's **sales revenue** of a change in price depends on the price elasticity of demand for its product.

250 The **cost of goods sold** is defined as the total of the material costs, labor costs, and overhead costs.

251 **Gross profit** is a key analytical tool in assessing a firm's operating performance.

244 支払期限が延長されると、資金調達源がさらにふえるため、買掛金勘定がふくらむ。

245 固定負債には、たとえば返済期限が貸借対照表日付より12カ月を超える期日に予定される、金融機関からの長期借入れなどがある。

▶ 固定負債：通常の営業活動以外で発生する債務のうち 返済期日が１年以内に到来しないもの

246 資本金とは、株主による株式購入の結果としての投資を意味している。

247 資本剰余金は、普通株式の額面価格を超えて株主が投資した金額を指す。

▶ 資本剰余金：会社が新株発行を行った際に資本金として組み入れなかった部分

248 ほとんどの会社定款では、利益剰余金残高はその企業の配当金支払能力の上限を意味している。

▶ 利益剰余金：利益のうち分配せずに社内に留保した部分

249 価格の変化が企業の売上高にどのような影響をもたらすかは、その企業の製品に対する需要の価格弾力性による。

250 売上原価とは、材料費・労務費・経費の合計である。

251 売上総利益は、企業の営業実績を評価する主要分析ツールである。

252 A company's **selling, general, and administrative expenses** are influenced by the operating activities it has to undertake to implement its competitive strategy.

253 **Depreciation** is an allocation of a fixed asset's cost to expense over the asset's useful life.

254 **Operating income** shows how the company has done in running its core business operations.

255 **Non-operating income** includes income from non-trading operations, such as refund of tax, interest and dividend received.

256 The effect of non-operating items is often referred to as the interest effect or interest burden because for many companies the interest expense is the primary **non-operating expense**.

257 When the assets of a company are relatively new, its reported **pre-tax profit** is likely to exceed its taxable income.

258 Most firms pay out some of their **net income** as dividends and reinvest, or retain, the rest.

259 **EBITDA** permits a more transparent comparison between the profitability of different firms because it is not distorted by factors such as differing depreciation policies.

252 企業の販売費および一般管理費は、競争戦略を実行するために取り組むべき営業活動により影響を受ける。

253 減価償却は、耐用年数にわたり固定資産の費用を配分するものである。

▶ 減価償却：固定資産の取得に要した支出を、その資産が使用できる期間に分割して費用計上する手続

254 営業利益は、その企業がコアビジネスをどのように運営してきたかを示すものである。

255 営業外収益には、税金の還付や利子、受取配当金などの商取引以外の活動から発生する収益がある。

256 営業外損益項目のもたらす影響は、しばしば金利影響または金利負担と呼ばれる。多くの企業にとって、支払利息が主な営業外費用であるからだ。

257 会社の資産が比較的新しい場合、計上された税引前利益が課税所得を上回ることが多い。

258 たいていの企業は、税引後利益の一部を配当金として支払い、残りを再投資あるいは留保する。

259 EBITDA は、減価償却方法の相違等の要因による影響を取り除けるため、異なる企業間における収益性の比較がより透明化できる。

▶ EBITDA：利払い前・税引前・減価償却前・その他償却前利益

260 If the company is seeking a line of credit, the bank is very likely to want a **cash flow** projection.

261 **Free cash flows** are available for distribution to all of the company's investors, including creditors and stockholders.

262 A company's net income and **operating cash flow** are seldom equal. A major difference between the two amounts is depreciation and amortization expenses.

263 It is typical for the **investing cash flow** section to be negative if the organization is growing and expanding its facilities.

264 Components of **financing cash flow** include inflows from additional borrowing and equity financing, and outflows for repayment of debt, dividend payments, and equity repurchases.

265 As the level of sales varies seasonally, short-term borrowings fluctuate with the level of seasonal **working capital**.

266 The accuracy of the **earnings forecast** is the most significant factor in projecting cash flows.

267 Stock price reaction to **earnings announcements** is related to both the sign and magnitude of unexpected earnings.

260 企業が融資枠を申請する場合、銀行は**キャッシュフロー**予測を求める可能性がきわめて高い。

261 **フリーキャッシュフロー**は、債権者や株主を含む企業のすべての投資家への配分に利用できる。

▶ フリーキャッシュフロー：通常の営業活動とその維持に必要な投資活動により生み出せるキャッシュフロー

262 企業の純利益と**営業キャッシュフロー**が一致することはめったにない。両者の主な違いは、減価償却費にある。

▶ operating cash flow=cash flow from operating activities

263 組織が成長を続け、設備を拡大中の場合、**投資キャッシュフロー**項目がマイナスになるのは珍しいことではない。

▶ investing cash flow=cash flow from investing activities

264 **財務キャッシュフロー**は、追加借入れや自己資本調達による現金流入と、債務返済や配当金払い、自社株買いによる現金流出とで構成されている。

▶ financing cash flow=cash flow from financing activities

265 売上水準は季節により変動するので、短期借入金は季節**運転資金**の水準に応じて変動する。

▶ 運転資金：企業が日々の営業を行うために必要な資金

266 正確な**収益見通し**は、資金繰り予測における最も重要な要素である。

267 **決算発表**に対する株価反応は、期待外利益の（正負の）状態と大きさの双方に関連する。

13　財務諸表

14 Accounting

268 In 2005, the accounting standards board of Japan decided to work on the convergence of Japanese GAAP with **IFRS**.

269 While unrealized price increases and decreases of available-for-sale securities are not reflected on the income statement, they are reported on the **statement of comprehensive income**.

270 The purpose of **comprehensive income** is to show the change in net assets from all sources other than investment by owners.

271 Under **book-value** accounting, assets and liabilities are recorded at historical cost, and capital is not adjusted for subsequent changes in their true market values.

272 **Acquisition cost** is reliable in the sense that accountants can verify the acquisition cost by reference to contracts and invoices.

273 If no market price is available, a valuation pricing model may be used to estimate **fair value**.

274 An **impairment loss** for property, plant, and equipment is recognized if book value is greater than the recoverable amount.

14 会　計

268 2005年、日本の企業会計基準委員会（ASBJ）は、J-GAAP（日本の会計基準）とIFRS（国際財務報告基準）とのコンバージェンス（統合）へ取り組むことを決定した。

269 売却可能有価証券の未実現保有損益は、損益計算書には反映されないが、包括利益計算書には計上される。

270 包括利益の目的は、出資者の投資を除いたすべての財源による純資産の変動を示すことである。

▶ 包括利益：純利益に土地や有価証券の含み益を加算した利益

271 簿価会計では、資産と負債は取得原価で記録され、資本が時価に基づく価格変動に応じて調整されることはない。

272 取得原価は、会計士が契約書や請求書類を参照することにより証明される価格であるという意味で、信頼性がある。

273 参照できる市場価格がない場合、価格評価モデルを用いて公正価値を算定することができる。

274 帳簿価額が回収可能価額を超える場合に、有形固定資産の減損損失が認識される。

▶ 減損損失：固定資産の収益性の低下により投資額の回収が見込めなくなった際に損失処理することにより発生する損失

275 The concept of **consolidated financial statements** is based on the assumption that a group of enterprises can be treated as a single accounting entity.

276 Before consolidated accounting was introduced in Japan, subsidiary companies were forced to buy goods from their **parent company** to increase the revenue of the parent company.

277 When one business owns the whole of another business, or has effective control of it, the latter business is a **subsidiary** of the former.

278 The equity method of accounting is used for investments in **affiliated companies**.

279 In the consolidated balance sheet, **minority interest** is the amount of equity investment made by outside shareholders to consolidated subsidiaries.

280 **Goodwill** represents the amount of the purchase price paid in excess of the market value of the individual net assets when a business is purchased.

281 One objective of **accounting for income taxes** is to recognize the amount of taxes payable or refundable for the current year.

282 **Deferred tax assets** should be recognized only to the extent that they can be recovered in the future.

275 連結財務諸表という概念は、企業グループが単一の会計主体として扱われるという想定に基づいている。

276 日本で連結会計が導入される前、子会社は親会社の収入をふやすために、その親会社の商品購入を強制されていた。

277 １事業体が他の事業体の全体を所有、または実質的な支配下に置く場合、後者は前者の子会社である。

278 持分法会計は、関連会社への投資に対して用いられる会計手法である。

279 連結貸借対照表では、少数株主持分とは連結子会社に対する外部株主による資本出資分のことである。

▶ 少数株主持分：子会社の自己資本のうち親会社が所有していない持分

280 営業権（のれん）は、１事業体が譲渡される際に、各純資産の市場価格を超えて支払われる購入金額を意味する。

▶ 営業権（のれん）：企業が有するブランド力、技術、ノウハウなどの無形の財産的価値

281 税効果会計の目的の１つは、年度中における未払いおよび還付税額を認識することである。

▶ 税効果会計：企業会計と税務会計の違いを調整し、税金費用を適切に期間配分する会計手続

282 繰延税金資産は、将来回収可能な範囲で認められるべきである。

▶ 繰延税金資産：税金の前払分を表す勘定科目

283 In an **operating lease**, the lessee generally has the right to cancel the lease and return the asset to the lessor.

284 A **financial lease** normally lasts for the entire economic life of the asset.

285 The **clean surplus** theory assumes ideal conditions in capital markets, including dividend irrelevancy.

15 Financial Analysis

286 The **current ratio** represents a company's ability to meet expected demands for cash.

287 The **acid-test ratio** is designed to measure how well a company can meet its obligations without having to liquidate its inventory.

288 A high **equity ratio** indicates that the firm has a financial cushion to pay back creditors in the event of a business downturn.

289 A company with a high **debt-to-equity ratio** is more likely to retain profits to ensure that it will have the funds to pay interest and principal on debt.

283 **オペレーティングリース**では、借主は通常、リースを解約し、資産を貸し手に返却する権利を有する。

284 **ファイナンスリース**は、通常、経済的耐用年数の全期間にわたり継続する。

285 **クリーンサープラス**理論は、配当無関連説も含めて、資本市場における理想的な状態を想定している。

15　財務分析

286 **流動比率**は、予測される資金需要を満たす企業の支払能力を示している。

▶ 流動比率：流動資産の流動負債に対する比率

287 **当座比率**は、在庫を処分する必要のない状態での、企業の支払能力を測る仕組みである。

▶ 当座比率：当座資産（すぐに現金化できる資産）の流動負債に対する比率

288 **自己資本比率**の高さは、企業が景気後退期に債権者へ返済可能な財務上の蓄えがあることを示している。

▶ 自己資本比率《一般事業会社》：自己資本の総資産に対する比率

289 **負債比率（D/Eレシオ）**が高い企業は、負債に対する利息および元金支払資金を確保するため、利益を留保する傾向が強い。

▶ 負債比率（D/Eレシオ）：負債の自己資本に対する比率

290 A too-high **leverage ratio** indicates excessive indebtedness, signaling the possibility the firm will be unable to earn enough to satisfy the obligations in its bonds.

291 The larger the proportion of debt used to finance a firm, the greater its **financial risk**.

292 Accounting insolvency occurs when a firm has **negative net worth** on its balance sheet.

293 Since the late 1990s, Japanese companies have put priority in repaying **interest-bearing liabilities**, refraining from capital investments.

294 **Interest coverage ratio** measures the debt servicing capacity of a firm to pay the interest on long-term loan.

295 Japanese firms' management, as symbolized by low **return on assets**, has not necessarily been efficient.

296 From the stockholders' point of view, the **return on equity** is a useful measure of performance.

297 In stable industries, such as groceries, one can expect to find the same **gross profit margin** from year to year.

290 あまりにも高い**レバレッジ比率**は、過度な負債を意味し、企業が債務返済義務を満たすのに十分な収益をあげられない可能性を示唆する。

▶ レバレッジ比率：総資産の自己資本に対する比率

291 企業への融資に用いられる負債の比率が高まれば高まるほど、当該企業の**財務リスク**は増す。

▶ 財務リスク：資金調達にあたって負債を用いることにより発生するリスク

292 会計上の破産は、企業が貸借対照表上で**債務超過**を抱えた際に生じる。

▶ 債務超過：負債が資産を上回っている状態

293 1990年代後半以後、日本企業は設備投資を控えつつ、**有利子負債**の返済を優先してきた。

294 **インタレストカバレッジレシオ**は、企業の長期負債に対する利払能力を測る指標である。

▶ インタレストカバレッジレシオ：(営業利益＋受取利息・配当金) ÷支払利息・手形売却損

295 日本の企業経営は、**ROA（総資産利益率）** の低さで象徴されるように、必ずしも効率的ではない。

296 株主の立場からみると、**ROE（自己資本利益率）** は業績をみる有効な尺度である。

297 食料品のような安定産業においては、毎年変わらぬ**売上総利益率**を期待できる。

298 The asset **turnover ratio** indicates how efficiently a company uses its assets to generate sales.

299 The longer the inventory **turnover period** the more financing is required by the company.

300 One of the factors behind low **labor productivity** in the Japanese service sector is that IT investment has not fully led to an improvement in productivity.

301 **Labor share** was especially hovering at a high level in the latter half of the 1990s due to stagnation of the Japanese economy as a whole.

302 High fixed costs force a high **capacity utilization rate** to maintain profitability.

303 A company with a high **break-even point** is quite vulnerable to economic declines.

304 Firms with greater amounts of **variable costs** as opposed to fixed costs will be less sensitive to business conditions.

305 If **fixed costs** are high, then a slight drop in sales can lead to large decline in EBIT.

298 資産回転率は、企業が売上げを生み出すのにどれだけ効率的に資産を活用しているかを示す。

▶ 回転率：資本や設備などが売上高などをどれだけ生み出しているかを測る指標

299 在庫回転期間が長ければ長いほど、企業はより多くの資金調達を必要とする。

▶ 回転期間：商品などの売上代金が現金で回収されるまでの期間

300 日本のサービス部門における労働生産性の低さの要因は、１つには、IT 投資が十分に生産性の改善をもたらさなかった点があげられる。

▶ 労働生産性：労働量１単位当りの生産量

301 労働分配率は、特に1990年代の後半に、日本経済全体の停滞を受けて高い割合が続いた。

▶ 労働分配率：付加価値のうち人件費の占める割合

302 固定費が高いと、収益性を維持するためには高い設備稼働率を強いられる。

▶ 設備稼働率：生産能力に対する実際の生産量の比率

303 損益分岐点が高い企業は、景気減速の影響をきわめて受けやすい。

304 固定費に対して変動費を多く抱える企業は、景気の影響を受けにくい。

305 固定費が高いと、わずかな売上げの低下で EBIT（税引前利払前利益）が大きく減少する。

306 **Marginal revenue** for a competitive firm is simply the market price.

307 When marginal revenue equals **marginal cost**, profit will be at its maximum.

308 Common stock dilution occurs when a common stock issuance results in an **earnings per share** decline.

309 **Book value per share** shows the value of the company's assets that each shareholder theoretically would receive if a company were liquidated.

310 The **price earnings ratio** measures how many years it would take the company at its current level of earnings to equal the market value.

311 A **price-book value ratio** of less than one indicates the liquidation value of the company is greater than the price of the stock.

16 Corporate Finance

312 Replacing non-risky with risky assets does not change **enterprise value**, but it does transfer value from creditors to shareholders.

313 The optimal capital structure is the mix of debt and equity that minimizes the **cost of capital**.

306 競争企業の限界収入は、単純に市場価格である。

▶ 限界収入：生産・販売量の増加に対する収入の増加分

307 限界収入と限界費用が等しい場合、利益は最大になる。

▶ 限界費用：生産・販売量の増加に対する費用の増加分

308 普通株の希薄化は、普通株発行により EPS（1株当り利益）が低下する場合に生じる。

309 BPS（1株当り純資産）は、企業の清算時に各株主が理論上受け取ることになるであろう企業の資産価値を示している。

310 PER（株価収益率）は、企業が現在の収益水準で市場価値に等しくなるまでに何年かかるかをみる指標だ。

311 PBR（株価純資産倍率）が1未満である場合、株価よりも会社の清算価値のほうが大きいことを示している。

16　コーポレートファイナンス

312 無リスク資産（安全資産）をリスク資産（危険資産）に換えても企業価値は変わらないが、価値は債権者から株主へと移動する。

313 最適資本構成とは、資本コストを最小にするような負債と資本の組合せである。

▶ 資本コスト：企業の資金調達に伴う費用

314 The **cost of debt** is simply the interest rate the firm must pay on new borrowing.

315 The **cost of equity** is normally higher than the cost of debt, as equity shareholders have to undertake a higher degree of risk.

316 The **WACC** is the overall return the firm must earn on its existing assets to maintain the value of its stock.

317 A company maximizes shareholder wealth by accepting only projects that have a positive **net present value**.

318 If the **internal rate of return** is equal to or greater than the required rate of return, then the project is considered acceptable.

319 The ratio of **capital expenditure** to depreciation does give an indication of the replacement rate of new for old assets.

320 Most **debt financing** comes from the keiretsu's main bank or from affiliated financial institutions.

321 Firms in the United States and United Kingdom use relatively more **equity financing** than firms in France, Germany, and Japan.

314 **負債コスト**は、単純に、新規借入れに対して支払義務のある金利のことである。
> ▶ 負債コスト：企業の負債による資金調達に伴う費用

315 **株主資本コスト**は通常、負債コストよりも高い。それは、株主がより高いリスクを受け入れなければならないからである。
> ▶ 株主資本コスト：企業の株式による資金調達に伴う費用

316 **WACC（加重平均資本コスト）**は、企業が株式の価値を維持するために達成すべき既存資産の利回り全体のことである。
> ▶ WACC（加重平均資本コスト）：負債コストと株主資本コストの加重平均

317 企業は、**NPV（正味現在価値）**がプラスとなるようなプロジェクトのみを選ぶことによって株主の富を最大化できる。

318 **IRR（内部収益率）**が要求利益率と等しいか、もしくはこれを上回る場合、そのプロジェクトは受入れ可能と判断される。
> ▶ IRR（内部収益率）：投資案件の利回りの一種

319 減価償却資産に対する**資本的支出**の比率は、新規資産の旧資産に対する置換比率を示すものである。
> ▶ 資本的支出：設備投資に係る支出

320 **デットファイナンス**の多くは、系列メインバンクか関連の金融機関からのものである。
> ▶ デットファイナンス：借入金や普通社債による資金調達

321 米国や英国の企業では、フランスやドイツ、日本と比べて、比較的多くの**エクイティファイナンス**の手法がとられる。
> ▶ エクイティファイナンス：株式による資金調達

322 Over these decades, Japanese companies increasingly shifted toward **direct financing** from capital markets.

323 In Japan, **indirect financing** from banks and insurance companies was dominant until the 1980s.

324 Japan abolished initial **minimum capital requirement** entirely in its Companies Act of 2005.

325 In many cases, the stock price fluctuates widely just before and after **capital increase**.

326 **Rights offers** protect existing shareholders from underpricing.

327 A **stock split** is conceptually similar to a stock dividend, but it is commonly expressed as a ratio.

328 An **initial public offering** is commonly used not only to obtain new funding but also to offer some founders and VC funds a way to cash out their investment.

329 The stock price reaction to a **seasoned equity offering** is negative on average.

330 Unlisted securities tend to be **private placements** where tradability or liquidity are not of significant importance to the issuer/investor.

322 この数十年の間に、日本企業（の資金調達手法）は、資本市場からの**直接金融**へと転換が進んだ。

▶ 直接金融：借り手と貸し手が直接資金を融通する方法

323 日本では1980年代まで、銀行や保険会社からの**間接金融**が主流であった。

▶ 間接金融：資金の融通において金融機関が仲介する方法

324 日本は2005年の会社法により、当初の**最低資本金制度**を撤廃した。

325 多くのケースにおいて、株価は**増資**の直前直後に大きく変動する。

326 **ライツオファリング（新株予約権無償割当て）**は、既存株主を株価下落から守る仕組みだ。

327 **株式分割**は、概念上は株式配当と同様であるが、一般的に比率で表される。

328 **IPO（新規株式公開）**は、一般的に、新規の資金調達目的のみならず、創業者やベンチャーキャピタルに投資回収の機会を提供することにも用いられる。

329 **SEO（公募増資）**に対して株価は平均的にマイナスの反応を示す。

330 非上場証券は**私募**になる傾向があり、そこでは取引可能性や流動性という点は発行人・投資家ともには特に重要視されない。

331 **Rights issues** refer to the selling of new shares on a pro rata basis to the existing shareholders.

332 It is well known that Japanese manufacturing firms make extensive use of **trade credit** in interfirm transactions.

333 Under the **offer for sale** method, the equity base of the company does not increase since no new shares are being issued.

334 The **cash dividend** is perhaps the most direct and immediate manner in which a company can return cash to shareholders.

335 Generally, a stock with a high **dividend yield** indicates that the stock's company is stable and not reinvesting its earnings.

336 Most firms that issue dividends try to maintain a consistent **dividend payout ratio**.

337 **Share repurchases**, like dividends, are a way to hand cash back to shareholders.

338 **Treasury stock** is not an asset and is not counted as either paid-in capital or as outstanding shares.

331 株主割当発行とは、新株を比例配分ベースで既存株主に売ることをいう。

▶ 株主割当発行：既存株主に持株数に応じて新株の引受け権を割り当てる株式発行方法

332 日本の製造企業が企業間取引において企業間信用をおおいに活用することはよく知られている。

▶ 企業間信用：企業相互間における融通

333 売出発行方式では、新株発行を伴わないため、企業の株主資本はふえない。

▶ 売出：不特定多数の投資家に対して既発の有価証券を売り付けること

334 現金配当は、企業が株主に現金を還元できるおそらく最も直接的で即時的な方法であろう。

335 一般的に、配当利回りの高い株式は、その企業が安定しており、収益を再投資に回していないことを意味する。

▶ 配当利回り：株価に対する配当金の比率

336 配当を出す企業のほとんどが、配当性向を一貫して維持しようと努めるものである。

▶ 配当性向：純利益に対する配当金の比率

337 自社株買いは、配当と同様に、現金を株主に還元する手法である。

338 金庫株は、資産とはみなされず、払込資本や発行済株式数として計上されない。

▶ 金庫株：自社株として取得しても消却せずにそのまま保有する株式

339 The right to attend the **shareholders' meeting** is one of the most important rights of the shareholder.

340 **Stable shareholders** are interested in control, not in dividends. Hence, dividends were kept low in Japanese corporations.

341 In Japan, the **main bank** is both a creditor and a stable shareholder for firms.

342 **Project finance** has been used to fund large-scale natural resource and infrastructure projects, such as pipelines, oil fields, mines, toll roads and power plants.

343 Many companies are able to arrange **debtor-in-possession** financing from commercial banks and other lenders immediately after filing for reorganization.

344 **Self-financing** avoids the need for perpetual interest payments on debentures or other permanent debts.

345 A **tracking stock** offers the parent company the advantage of maintaining control over a separated subsidiary.

346 Japanese corporations began to unwind some of their **cross-shareholdings** in the early 1990s.

339 株主総会に出席する権利は、株主の最も重要な権利の1つである。

340 安定株主は配当よりも支配に関心を向けている。それゆえに、日本企業では配当は低く維持されていた。

341 日本では、メインバンクは企業にとって債権者でもあり安定株主でもある。

342 プロジェクトファイナンスは、パイプラインや油田、鉱山、有料道路、発電所などの大規模な天然資源やインフラ計画への融資として用いられてきた。

▶ プロジェクトファイナンス：特定のプロジェクトを対象とした融資

343 多くの企業が、会社更生法の適用申請直後に、商業銀行やその他の貸し手からのDIPファイナンスを受けることができる。

▶ DIPファイナンス：民事再生法などの倒産手続開始後の企業に対する融資

344 自己金融では、債券やその他長期負債の無期限の利息払いの必要性がない。

▶ 自己金融：内部留保や減価償却により自社内で資金調達すること

345 トラッキングストックは、親会社に、独立した子会社に対する支配力を維持できる利点を与える。

▶ トラッキングストック：利益配当が企業業績でなく特定部門や子会社の業績に連動する株式

346 日本企業は、1990年代の初めに、株式持合いの一部を解消し始めた。

347 In undertaking a **debt for equity swap**, banks become shareholders in the company, as well as generally remaining lenders to it.

348 **Hybrid securities** have characteristics of both debt and equity and often are a combination of traditional and derivative financial instruments.

17 Bank Loan

349 Because of the stop of expansion in capital demand and the developments in interest liberalization, the margin in the bank **loan business** has generally declined.

350 The sharp decrease in output growth in Japan in the early 1990s left many firms unable to repay their **bank loans**.

351 The Japanese **banking system** is characterized by a small number of large, internationally active major banks and a large number of regional banks.

352 The Japanese banks at the end of fiscal year 1997 had **outstanding loans** of about 500 trillion yen.

353 The **prime rate** is often defined as the interest rate charged by a commercial bank to its most creditworthy customers.

347 デットエクイティスワップ（債務の株式化）では、銀行はその企業の株主となると同時に、通常、その企業の貸し手であり続ける。

348 ハイブリッド証券は債務と自己資本の双方の特質を有しており、金融商品としては、しばしば従来的金融商品と金融派生商品組合せの場合がある。

17　銀行借入れ

349 資金需要の拡張が止まり、金利自由化が進んだために、銀行の融資業務の利益は全般的に減少している。

350 1990年代初めに日本では経済成長率が急激に低下し、多くの企業が銀行借入れの返済ができなくなった。

351 日本の銀行制度は、少数の国際的にも活動を広げる大手都市銀行と多数の地方銀行に特徴づけられる。

352 1997年の会計年度末の時点で、日本では銀行の貸付残高が約500兆円であった。

353 最優遇貸出金利は、商業銀行による最も信用力の高い顧客を対象とした利率としばしば定義づけられる。

▶ 最優遇貸出金利：金融機関が最も信用度の高い企業に融資する際に適用する金利

354 While **collateral** reduces the bank's risk, it increases the costs of lending and monitoring.

355 **Loan on deeds** is utilized for a long-term loan with a period exceeding a year.

356 Under the **loans on bills** arrangement, banks can always sell their holdings of bills in the secondary market.

357 **Overdraft loans** are loans that carry a commitment by banks to provide loans up to a pre-specified ceiling.

358 The best-known and most common form of loan is a **term loan** arranged between a borrower and a single bank.

359 Firms use **commitment line** contracts with banks to prepare for funding emergencies.

360 The **syndicated loan** affords borrowers access to large amounts of money that single lenders cannot supply.

361 One advantage of a **line of credit** is that it offers easy and immediate access to funds during tight money market conditions.

362 The magnitude of **nonperforming loans** on Japanese banks' balance sheets rose to 7% of GDP in the year 2000.

354 担保は、銀行のリスクを軽減するものの、貸付とモニタリングの費用が増額になる。

355 証書貸付は、1年を超える長期ローンに利用される。

356 手形貸付の取引の取決めのもとで、銀行は常時、自らの保有手形を流通市場にて売却できる。

357 当座貸越とは、あらかじめ設定した限度額まで銀行が融資を提供することを約束した融資のことである。

358 最もよく知られる一般的な貸付は、借り手と単一銀行間で交わされるタームローンである。

▶ タームローン：金利や期限など条件を定めて行う証書貸付

359 企業は、銀行とのコミットメントライン契約を利用して、緊急融資に備える。

▶ コミットメントライン：一定の融資枠の範囲内で顧客の請求に基づき金融機関が融資を行うこと

360 協調融資は、単一の貸し手では供給できない多額の資金を借り手が利用できる手段を提供する。

361 信用与信枠の利点の1つは、金融市場が逼迫している時期でも簡潔で迅速な資金調達が得られるという点である。

▶ 信用与信枠：金融機関が取引先に対して設定する融資の限度額

362 日本の銀行のバランスシート上の不良債権額は、2000年にはGDPの7％にまでふくれあがった。

363 The **credit crunch** mostly affected small businesses, which were unable to obtain bank loans.

364 In a **universal banking** system, banks are permitted to carry out a wide variety of financial and nonfinancial activities.

365 **Wholesale banking** concentrates on providing financial services to large corporations and government agencies.

366 Banks now have come to realize the profitability of the **retail banking** market, especially its income from transaction fees.

367 As in the United States, Japan also eliminated the separation of **investment banking** and commercial banking.

18 Credit Risk

368 The difference in the expected **probability of default** between AA− and A+, for example, is not necessarily equal to that between BB− and B+.

369 In addition to diversifying funding sources, securitization as an asset disposition vehicle allows the financial institution to diversify **credit risk**.

363 銀行の貸渋りの影響を受けたのはほとんどが小企業で、銀行融資を受けることができなかった。

364 ユニバーサルバンキング制度のもとでは、銀行はあらゆる金融活動も非金融活動も実施することが許されている。

> ▶ ユニバーサルバンキング：単一の金融機関が貸付業務、証券業務、信託業務など広範な業務を行うことができる銀行業務の形態

365 ホールセールバンキングは、大手企業や政府関連機関への金融サービスに集中している。

> ▶ ホールセールバンキング：金融機関の大口顧客との金融取引

366 銀行は、リテールバンキング市場、特にその取引手数料収入の収益性をいまや実現している。

> ▶ リテールバンキング：金融機関の主に個人顧客との小口金融取引

367 米国のように、日本でも投資銀行業務と商業銀行業務の仕切りを排除した。

> ▶ 投資銀行業務：企業の資金調達やM&Aなどのサポートを行う業務

18　信用リスク

368 AA－とA＋との間の期待デフォルト確率における差は、BB－とB＋の差と必ずしも同じとは限らない。

369 資金調達源の分散のほかに、資産処分のビークル（手段）としての証券化で金融機関は信用リスクを分散することができる。

370 During the 2007-2009 financial crisis **credit spreads** widened to near-record levels.

371 **Corporate bond spread** variability implies that these bonds may be more volatile than government bonds.

372 In the wake of the financial crisis, **counterparty risk** increased rapidly as the respective counterparties were not able to pay their obligations.

373 **Rating agencies** aim to offer an independent credit opinion to investors, based on a set of objective and precise criteria.

374 A company's **credit rating** determines the interest rate it must pay.

375 **External ratings** improve the efficiency of the market, lowering costs for investors and debt issuers.

376 A credit **rating upgrade** in a company's debt may be a reflection of a general upturn in its industrial sector.

377 The increase in debt-to-capital ratio and a decrease in earnings lead to a **rating downgrade**.

378 BBB and above is classified as **investment grade**, while BB and below is characterized as speculative grade.

370 2007年から2009年の金融危機の時期には、信用スプレッドが新記録に近いレベルまで広がった。

▶ 信用スプレッド：社債の国債に対する金利上乗せ幅のうち信用リスクに見合う部分

371 社債スプレッドの変動性をみると、国債よりも社債のほうが変動が激しい可能性があることがうかがえる。

▶ 社債スプレッド：社債の国債に対する金利上乗せ幅（信用スプレッドに流動性スプレッドを加えたもの）

372 金融危機の結果として、それぞれの取引先が債務を弁済できないので、取引先リスクが急速に増大した。

373 格付機関は、客観的かつ精密な基準に基づいて、投資家に独自のクレジットオピニオンを提供することを目的としている。

374 ある企業が支払うべき金利はその企業の信用格付で決まる。

375 外部格付は、投資家や起債者のコストを軽減して、市場の効率を向上させる。

376 企業の債務における格上げは、その産業部門における全般的な好転を反映している場合もある。

377 負債資本比率の上昇と収益の減少は格下げにつながる。

378 BBB以上の等級は投資適格レベルに分類されるが、BB以下は、投機的等級と位置づけられる。

379 For **speculative grade** companies, investors are more concerned about the recovery prospects in the event of default.

380 A **split rating** may occur because one rating agency places a different emphasis on certain variables.

19 Securitization

381 **Securitization** can be represented as transference of risk to the capital markets.

382 Generally, the senior-subordinated structure used on **securitized products** in Japan contains few tranches.

383 **Mezzanine finance** is an intermediate stage between senior debt and equity finance in relation to both risk and return.

384 An advantage of **factoring** is that the company selling its receivables immediately receives cash for operating and other needs.

379 投機的格付の会社の場合、投資家は債務不履行が起きたときの回収見通しについてより関心が高い。

380 ある格付機関が特定の変数に対し別の見解を示すために、スプリットレーティングが起きる可能性がある。

▶ スプリットレーティング：格付機関による格付の格差

19 証券化

381 証券化は、資本市場へのリスクの転移であるといえる。

▶ 証券化：企業等が保有する資産等を裏付けにして有価証券を発行し資金調達する手法

382 一般的に、日本において証券化商品に使用されている優先劣後構造には、トランシェはほとんどない。

383 メザニンファイナンスは、リスクとリターンに関してはシニア債務とエクイティファイナンスの中間に位置するファイナンス手法である。

▶ メザニンファイナンス：デットファイナンスとエクイティファイナンスの中間に位置するファイナンス手法

384 ファクタリングの利点は、売掛債権を売る会社が、営業やその他の用途に即時現金を受け取れることである。

▶ ファクタリング：ファクタリング会社が企業から売掛債権を買い取り債権回収の代行を行う取引

385 The creditworthiness of the **asset-backed securities** is independent of the creditworthiness of the company that originally owned the underlying assets.

386 The most common type of **asset-based lending** is backed by receivables or inventory lines.

387 **Asset-backed commercial paper** is commercial paper issued by either corporations or large financial institutions through a bankruptcy-remote special purpose corporation.

388 The asset pool of most **collateralized debt obligation** comprises debt issued by more than 100 different borrowers.

389 **Collateralized loan obligations** are financed with several tranches of debt that have rights to the collateral and payment stream in descending order.

390 **Collateralized bond obligations** are backed by a portfolio of secured or unsecured senior or junior bonds issued by a variety of corporate or sovereign obligors.

391 The main innovation of the **collateralized mortgage obligations** is that it provides investors with a steady stream of income for a predictable term.

385 ABS（資産担保証券）の信用度は、原資産をもともと所有していた企業の信用度とは無関係である。

▶ ABS（資産担保証券）：貸付債権等の資産を裏付けとして発行される証券

386 ABL（資産担保融資）の最も一般的なタイプは、売上債権や在庫品を担保としている。

387 ABCP（資産担保コマーシャルペーパー）は、企業や大手金融機関によって、親会社の破産の影響が及ばない（倒産隔離）SPC（特別目的会社）を通じて発行されるコマーシャルペーパーである。

388 ほとんどのCDO（債務担保証券）の資産プールは、100を超える異なる借り手により出された債務で構成されている。

389 CLO（ローン担保証券）は、担保と支払流列に対する権利を降順で有する複数の債務トランシェを通じて資金調達される。

390 CBO（社債担保証券）は、さまざまな企業もしくはソブリン債務者によって発行された、担保付もしくは無担保のシニア債もしくはジュニア債のポートフォリオで裏付けされている。

391 CMO（不動産抵当証券担保債券）の最も革新的な点は、想定された期間は、投資家たちに着実な収益をもたらすという点である。

392 In Japan, the early symptoms of the financial crisis were not so serious because Japanese financial institutions are relatively less exposed to **mortgage-backed securities**.

393 Within structured assets, **residential mortgage-backed securities** are the most prevalent asset type.

394 **Commercial mortgage-backed securities** are backed by mortgages on commercial real estate (e.g., office buildings, rental apartments, hotels).

395 **Pass-through certificates** are treated as owners of the trust and entitle holders to a pro rata share of principal and interest payments.

20 Corporate Governance & Employment

396 Japan's **corporate governance** system is often linked to that of Germany because banks can play an influential role in companies in both countries.

397 In 2000, Japan adopted new accounting rules that exposed the extent of pension underfunding in many **corporate pension** plans.

392 日本の金融機関は、MBS（不動産担保証券）のエクスポージャーが比較的少ないため、日本では金融危機の初期兆候は、さほど深刻ではなかった。

▶ MBS（不動産担保証券）：不動産担保融資を裏付けとして発行される証券

393 ストラクチャードアセットのなかでは、RMBS（住宅ローン担保証券）が最も普及している資産タイプである。

394 CMBS（商業不動産担保証券）は、商業不動産（オフィスビル、賃貸集合住宅、ホテルなど）の不動産担保を裏付けとしている。

395 パススルー証書は信託物の所有者として扱われ、保有者に元利金支払の比例配分を受け取る資格を与える。

▶ パススルー証書：ローンの元利金をそのまま証券を購入した投資家に支払うタイプの証券

20 コーポレートガバナンス・雇用

396 日本の企業統治（コーポレートガバナンス）システムは、ドイツのシステムと関連する面が多い。これは、どちらの国でも銀行が企業に対して影響力をもちうるからである。

397 2000年に日本は新しい会計基準を導入したが、これが多くの企業年金制度における積立不足の広がりを露呈することとなった。

398 In **defined benefit** plans, the employer bears the investment risk to fund the benefit.

399 In **defined contribution** plans, the employees decide how their contributions should be invested.

400 **Liability-driven investment** responds to the need to match the asset allocation of a pension scheme more closely with future liabilities.

401 **Stock options** are a way to tie an employee's compensation and motivation to the shareholders' interest.

402 In principle, Japanese **ESOPs** can function as a group incentive that aligns the interests of the firm and workers.

403 **Lifetime employment** was once conceived as a means of integration and socialization for each company recruit.

404 Many countries in the world have adopted a **minimum wage** that covers all or part of the wage-earning population.

398 **確定給付型年金**では、雇用者側は給付金拠出に対する投資リスクを負う。

▶ 確定給付型年金：年金受給額があらかじめ確定されている年金制度

399 **確定拠出年金**においては、従業員は自らが掛け金の運用方法を決定する。

▶ 確定拠出年金：掛け金の額は確定しているが受給額は加入者自身の運用結果に応じて決定する年金制度

400 **LDI（年金債務重視の運用）**は、年金スキームの資産配分をより将来の負債に近づける必要性に応える運用手法である。

401 **ストックオプション**は、従業員の報酬およびモチベーションと株主の利益とを結ぶ1つの方法である。

▶ ストックオプション：役職員があらかじめ定められた価額で会社の株式を取得できる権利

402 原則的には、日本の **ESOP（従業員持株制度）**は、会社と従業員の利益をマッチングするグループインセンティブとして機能しうる。

▶ ESOP（従業員持株制度）：企業が従業員に対して自社株式を報酬として付与する制度

403 **終身雇用**は、それぞれの企業の新入社員に対する企業との一体化と社会化の手段としてかつては考えられていた。

404 世界では、賃金所得層のすべてもしくは一部を対象として、多くの国が**最低賃金**を採用している。

405 The aim of **work-sharing** is to redistribute the total volume of work in the economy in order to increase employment opportunities for all those wishing to work.

406 The collapse of Enron, WorldCom, and other large corporations in 2001 and 2002 motivated Congress to pass the **Sarbanes-Oxley Act** of 2002.

21 Mergers and Acquisitions

407 One of the most fundamental motives for **mergers and acquisitions** is growth.

408 In a **statutory merger**, two or more companies combine such that only one of the companies remains in existence.

409 After a **consolidation**, the new corporation acquires all of the assets and liabilities of the corporations that were consolidated.

410 A **triangle merger** is a type of merger that uses a subsidiary corporation to acquire a target corporation.

405 ワークシェアリングの目的は、働く意欲のあるすべての人を対象に、雇用機会をふやすために経済枠内での全労働量を再分配することである。

▶ ワークシェアリング：従業員の労働時間を短縮することで雇用者数の増大を図ること

406 2001年と2002年のエンロン、ワールドコム、その他の大手企業の破綻が、米国議会での2002年サーベンスオクスリー（SOX）法案可決に拍車をかけた。

▶ サーベンスオクスリー（SOX）法：財務報告の正確性、内部統治の強化等を目的として成立した法律

21　M＆A

407 M&Aに対する最も基本的な動機の１つは企業の成長である。

408 吸収合併においては、合併企業のうちの１社のみが存続できるよう、複数の企業が結合する。

409 新設合併後に、新規企業は、合併した複数の企業のすべての資産および負債を得ることになる。

410 三角合併とは、対象会社を獲得する目的で子会社を利用するタイプの合併である。

411 Japan enacted a new "Company Law" with M&A provisions effective in 2007 that greatly reduced the regulatory barriers to foreign **acquisitions** of Japanese companies.

412 One of the advantages of an **asset acquisition** is that the bidder may not have to gain the approval of its shareholders.

413 The objective of a **horizontal merger** is to gain greater market share through economies of scale.

414 A **vertical merger** takes place along the value chain to reduce the overall cost of the product or service.

415 A **conglomerate** merger occurs when the companies are not competitors and do not have a buyer-seller relationship.

416 With a **holding company** structure, an acquirer may be able to attain control of a target for a much smaller investment than would be necessary in a 100% stock acquisition.

417 **Stock swap** is effective during business group restructuring between a parent company and a partially owned subsidiary company.

411 日本はM&A条項を盛り込んだ2007年施行の新会社法を制定した。これは、外国による日本企業買収の規制バリアを大幅に緩和したものである。

412 資産買収の利点の１つは、買収者が必ずしも株主の承認を得る必要がないということである。

413 水平合併の目的は、規模の経済によって、より大きなマーケットシェアを獲得することである。
> ▶ 水平合併：同業種の企業同士の合併

414 垂直合併は、製品もしくはサービスのコスト全体を軽減するためのバリューチェーン（価値連鎖）に沿って生じる。
> ▶ 垂直合併：異なる工程の業務を担う企業同士の合併

415 コングロマリット合併は、企業同士が競合相手でもなく、また売買関係にもない場合に起きる。
> ▶ コングロマリット：直接の関連をもたない多数の事業から形成される複合企業

416 持株会社方式であれば、100％の株式取得に必要な投資額よりもはるかに低い投資額で、取得企業はターゲット企業を支配できる可能性がある。
> ▶ 持株会社：他の会社を実質的に支配することを目的として設立する会社

417 株式交換は、親会社と一部出資の子会社の間の事業グループ再編の際に有効である。
> ▶ 株式交換：他社の完全親会社となるために、自社の株式と他社の全株式を交換する制度

418 **Stock transfer** is to establish a complete parent holding company, which will control various fully owned subsidiaries.

419 Mandatory **tender offers** are required in cases where purchases acquire more than 10% of the voting rights of a company.

420 A **horizontal integration** by the merger of two firms producing the same product also promotes monopoly.

421 **Vertical integration** should be considered from two viewpoints: internal benefits and costs, and effects on competitive posture.

422 Although there are several thousand takeovers annually in Japan, most of these are **friendly acquisitions** between related companies.

423 Because both Germany and Japan have a system of permanent large investors, **hostile takeovers** are rare in both countries.

424 Early studies showed that, on average, the adoption of a **poison pill** led to a decline in the company's stock price.

418 株式移転とは、個々の完全子会社を支配する完全親会社を設立することである。

419 企業の議決権の10%を超える株式取得には、強制的株式公開買付けが求められる。

▶ tender offer=takeover bid
▶ 株式公開買付け：不特定多数の株主から市場外で株式等を買い集める制度

420 同じ製品を生産する2つの会社の合併による水平統合は、独占も助長する。

▶ 水平統合：同一の工程で複数の企業グループが一体化すること

421 垂直統合は2つの観点から考えるべきである。すなわち、内部の便益と費用、それに競争上の地位への影響である。

▶ 垂直統合：自社の仕入先や販売先を統合して事業領域の拡張を行うこと

422 日本では、年間に何千もの買収がみられるが、ほとんどの場合は、関連会社間の友好的買収である。

423 ドイツと日本はどちらにも恒久的大口投資家のシステムがあるので、どちらの国でも敵対的買収はまれである。

424 概して、ポイズンピルの採用は会社の株価の下落につながるということが早くからの研究で示された。

▶ ポイズンピル：新株予約権を発行して買収する側の持株比率を下げる仕組み

425 A **white knight** launches a takeover bid involving a premium on the price of stock, thus not cheating the shareholders out of their profits from the initial hostile takeover bid.

426 Governments typically use **golden shares** to maintain a degree of control over privatized corporations.

427 **Corporate restructuring** is often warranted when the current structure of the corporation is not yielding values that are consistent with market or management's expectations.

428 In a **spin-off**, shares are issued on a pro rata basis and distributed to the parent company's shareholders, also on a pro rata basis.

429 In a **joint venture**, companies can enter into an agreement to provide certain resources toward the achievement of a particular business goal.

430 In a joint venture, a separate entity is often created, whereas in a **strategic alliance** the agreement and the relationship are less formal.

431 A **management buyout** is a means of transferring ownership from the founder to the management team.

425 ホワイトナイトは、株価にプレミアム（上乗せ価格）をつけて株式公開買付けを実施する。したがって、当初の敵対的公開買付けにより得た利益を株主から奪うということはない。

▶ ホワイトナイト：敵対的買収を仕掛けられた会社を、経営陣と合意のうえで友好的に買収する会社

426 民営化された企業に対し、ある程度の支配権を維持する目的で、政府は黄金株を利用するのが典型的だ。

▶ 黄金株：会社の合併などの重要議案を否決できる株式

427 企業再建とは、現在の企業構造が、市場もしくは経営陣の期待に即した利益を生んでいない場合にはおおむね実施する正当な理由があるものとみなされる。

428 スピンオフでは、株式は比例配分ベースで発行され、同じく比例配分ベースで親会社の株主に分配される。

▶ スピンオフ：親会社の一部の事業または子会社を独立した会社として切り離すこと

429 合弁事業では、諸企業は、ある特別なビジネスゴールの達成に向けてある程度の資金を提供する契約を交わすこともできる。

430 合弁事業では、別会社が創設されることがよくあるが、戦略的提携では、合意や提携関係は正式性が弱まる（関係がゆるい）。

▶ 戦略的提携：複数の企業が対等な立場で共同事業を推進すること

431 MBO（マネジメントバイアウト）は、創業者から経営陣へと所有権を移転するための手段である。

▶ MBO（マネジメントバイアウト）：経営陣による自社株式の買収

432 Most **leveraged buyouts** are buyouts of small and medium-sized companies or divisions of large companies.

433 Merger planners tend to look for cost-reducing synergies as the main source of **operating synergies**.

22 Industries

434 Japanese **manufacturing industry** accounts for over 90% of total exports.

435 The **food industry** is mainly characterized by a relatively large number of standard articles, small profits and quick returns.

436 Significant new developments have taken place in the **textile industry** to meet the changing consumer tastes and increasing environmental pressures.

437 **Chemical industry** produces a wide range of intermediate goods that are used by the chemical industry itself and a variety of end-user/customer industries.

432 LBO（レバレッジドバイアウト）は、中小企業や大企業の部門を買収するケースがほとんどである。

▶ LBO（レバレッジドバイアウト）：買収対象企業の資産あるいは将来キャッシュフローを担保にした負債を買収資金にして行う企業買収

433 合併の立案者は、コスト削減シナジーを主たる生産シナジー源として追求する傾向にある。

▶ 生産シナジー：生産手段や原材料の共有化などによる相乗効果

22　産　業

434 日本の製造業は全輸出の90％超を占める。

435 食品業界の主な特徴は、比較的多数の定番商品と、薄利多売である。

436 消費者の嗜好の変化と、増大する環境面での圧力に対応するべく、繊維業界では大幅な新規開発が行われてきた。

437 化学業界では、業界内での使用とさまざまなエンドユーザーや消費者業界の使用のために、いろいろな半製品が生産されている。

438 It is true that compared to other industries the **pharmaceutical industry** reinvests a higher percentage of profits in R&D.

439 Since **petroleum industry** is a capital-intensive industry, the aggregate employment is small compared to the production output.

440 Japan's **steel industry** has successfully maintained production levels by developing new products and by meeting customer demands.

441 Japan's **machinery industry** is characterized by a large number of small and medium factories employing the majority of industry workers.

442 The cost advantages of the Japanese **automobile industry** derive from lean production or lower vertical integration than in the North American and European automobile industry.

443 The international competitiveness of the Japanese **electrical and electronics industry** has been built on a high level of research and development.

444 The **consumer electronics industry** is characterized by severe pricing pressure resulting from overcapacity.

438 医薬品業界は、他の産業と比較すると、利益をR&D（研究開発）へ再投資する割合が高いのは事実である。

439 石油業界は資本集約的産業であるため、総雇用は、生産高と比較すると少ない。

440 日本の鉄鋼業界は、新製品の開発と顧客の需要に応えることによって、生産レベルをうまく維持してきた。

441 日本の機械業界は、産業労働者の大半を雇用する多数の中小規模工場に特徴づけられる。

442 日本の自動車業界のコスト優位性は、北米や欧州の自動車業界に比べて、リーン生産（生産の効率のよさ）、もしくは、垂直統合度の低さに由来する。

443 日本の電気電子業界の国際的競争力は、高レベルの研究開発の上に築かれた。

444 家電業界は、過剰生産能力に起因する厳しい価格圧力に特徴づけられる。

445 The **construction industry** is a typical order-receiving industry, and Japan's contractors are very numerous.

446 Unlike most industries, the **transportation industry** is not only large but highly diversified.

447 The **electric power industry** is often cited as an example of a natural monopoly, an industry in which only one company can be profitable.

448 The performance of the Japanese **wholesale industry** can be attributed to large general trading firms.

449 Companies in the **retail industry** tend to have high turnover ratio because of the highly competitive market.

450 The **real estate industry** benefited from its possession of rapidly appreciating land assets in Japan during the 1980s.

451 The ratio of non-regular employment is high in the **services industry**.

445 建設業界は受注産業の典型であり、日本では請負業者の数はおびただしく多い。

446 他のほとんどの産業とは違って、運輸業界は、大きいだけでなく、きわめて多様化している。

447 電力業界は、自然独占の典型としてよく取り上げられる。つまり、たった1つの会社が利益を得ることができる業界だということである。

448 日本の卸売業界の業績は、大手総合商社に帰因するといえる。

449 小売業界の企業は、非常に競合性の高い市場のために、回転率が高い傾向にある。

450 不動産業界は1980年代、日本国内で所有していた土地資産が急速に高騰したおかげで利益を得た。

451 臨時雇用者の割合は、サービス業界では高い。

第3章 金融

23 Financial Markets

452 As Japan became money-affluent and increased its presence in the international community, the financial system and **financial market** were increasingly liberalized and internationalized.

453 As open-market transactions sharply increased, Japan's **money market** grew in size.

454 A well-organized **capital market** is crucial for mobilizing both domestic and international capital.

455 When a corporation uses an IPO to raise capital, the stock is sold in the **primary market**.

456 Except for a small number of major issuers, liquidity of **secondary markets** for corporate bonds in developed countries is generally thin.

457 The creation of the **money stock** is determined by the interplay between the central bank, the commercial banks, and the non-bank private sector.

458 Quantitative easing pumped up the **monetary base** to an exceptionally high level of 22% of GDP, compared to a long-run average of about 8%.

459 In 2001, under quantitative easing, the BoJ's policy target was officially shifted from the level of call rate to the BoJ **checking account** balance.

23 金融市場

452 日本が金銭的に豊かになり、国際社会においてその存在力を増すにつれて、金融システムや金融市場は、ますます自由化と国際化が進んだ。

453 公開市場取引が急速に増加するにつれて、日本の短期金融市場は規模的に成長した。

454 十分に組織化された資本市場（長期金融市場）は、内外資本を流通させるためにきわめて重要である。

455 企業が資本調達目的でIPO（新規株式公開）を行うとき、株式は発行市場にて売りに出される。

456 少数の主要な発行者は別として、先進国での社債に対する流通市場の流動性は一般的に乏しい。

457 マネーストック（マネーサプライ）の創出は、中央銀行、商業銀行および民間非銀行部門の間での相互作用で決定される。

▶ マネーストック（マネーサプライ）：金融機関から経済全体に供給される貨幣量

458 量的金融緩和により、約8％という長期平均と比較して、対GDP比22％というまれにみる高水準にまでマネタリーベースが拡大した。

▶ マネタリーベース：中央銀行から民間金融機関に供給される貨幣量

459 2001年、量的緩和政策のもと、日本銀行の政策目標は、コールレート水準から日銀当座預金残高へと正式に置き換えられた。

▶ 当座預金：出し入れが自由な無利息の預金

460 **Negotiable certificates of deposit** can be redeemed at any time in the secondary market without loss of deposit funds to the bank.

461 **Commercial paper** is a method of short-term financing that is usually available only to large, well-known firms.

462 The **interbank market** makes up approximately 75% of all foreign exchange transactions.

463 Because of the expansion of **open markets**, such as the gensaki market and the CD market, arbitrage opportunities exist between the open markets and the interbank markets.

464 During the high-growth period the **financial surplus** in the household sector was used mostly to cover the financial deficit in the corporate sector.

465 The corporate sector reduced its **financial deficit** and the government sector widened its financial deficit.

466 An **offshore market** is different from the domestic market in that it provides free fundraising and investment transactions between nonresidents.

467 **Financial liberalization** may lead to a financial meltdown, as many Asian nations experienced in the 1997 crisis.

460 **譲渡性預金**は、銀行預金の損失を出すことなしに、流通市場にていつでも償還することができる。

▶ 譲渡性預金：他人への譲渡が可能な無記名の定期預金

461 **コマーシャルペーパー**は、通常大手有名企業のみが利用可能な短期の資金調達方法である。

▶ コマーシャルペーパー：企業が短期資金の調達を目的に発行する無担保の約束手形

462 全外国為替取引の約75%を**インターバンク市場**が占めている。

▶ インターバンク市場：取引参加者が金融機関に限定される短期金融市場

463 現先市場やCD（譲渡性預金）市場などの**オープン市場**の拡大により、オープン市場とインターバンク市場との間に裁定機会が存在する。

▶ オープン市場：金融機関以外に一般企業なども取引に参加できる短期金融市場

464 高度成長期に、家計部門での**資金余剰**は、ほとんどが企業部門の資金不足を補うために使われた。

465 企業部門は**資金不足**が減少し、政府部門は資金不足が拡大した。

466 **オフショア市場**は、非居住者間での自由な資金調達および投資取引を提供する点において、国内市場とは異なる。

▶ オフショア市場：国内の金融市場の法的制約を受けない国際金融市場

467 **金融自由化**は、多くのアジア諸国が1997年の危機で経験したように、金融崩壊を招く可能性がある。

468 The three areas of **market risk** are interest rate or reinvestment rate risk, equity or security price risk, and foreign exchange risk.

469 The longer the duration of the bond, the greater is the potential **interest rate risk**.

470 Emerging markets typically have higher **country risk** than developed countries.

471 In April 2009, concerns over Greek **sovereign risk** spilled over to other European countries.

472 Bid-ask spreads and trading volume are used to assess **liquidity risk**.

473 **Value at risk** measures the loss that will be exceeded with a specific probability such as 5%.

24 Financial Institutions

474 Many financial conglomerates are composed of various **financial institutions** that were originally independent.

468 市場リスクの３つの領域は、金利・再投資リスク、株式・証券価格リスクおよび、外国為替リスクである。

469 債券のデュレーションが長ければ長いほど、潜在的な金利リスクは大きくなる。

470 新興成長市場のほうが、概して先進国よりもカントリーリスクが高い。

471 2009年４月に、ギリシャのソブリンリスクの懸念が他の欧州諸国にまで波及した。

> ▶ソブリンリスク：政府や政府機関の借入れや債券が債務不履行となるリスク

472 ビッドアスクスプレッド（売値と買値の差）と売買高は流動性リスクを評価するために利用される。

473 バリューアットリスクは、５％などのように特定の確率で上回るであろう損失を計測する。

> ▶バリューアットリスク：市場リスク（想定される最大損失）を統計的に測定した数値

24　金融機関

474 多くの金融コングロマリットは、もともとは独立したさまざまな金融機関から構成されている。

475 During 1999, the Financial System Reform Law allowed **commercial banks** to own brokerage firms that underwrite equity and debt securities.

476 The important role of **regional banks** in supporting regional economic activity is a key rationale for their preferential treatment.

477 Since the law requires the separation of trust transactions from commercial banking, **trust banks** manage trust accounts and bank accounts separately.

478 **Investment banks** usually earn their income from fees charged to clients rather than from commissions on stock trades.

479 Many banks organize themselves into **bank holding companies** because they expect this organizational form to be more profitable than a simple bank would be.

480 The liberalization of brokerage commission triggered a price competition among **securities companies**.

481 **Asset management companies** earn their living mostly from the asset management fees that they charge their clients.

475 1999年、金融制度改革法で、**商業銀行**は、株式や債務証券を引き受ける仲買業者を所有することが可能になった。

476 **地方銀行**が地方の経済活動を支援するという重要な役割を担っている点が、彼らに対して優遇措置がとられる主な理論的根拠である。

477 法律では、信託取引を商業銀行から切り離すことが求められているため、**信託銀行**は信託勘定と銀行勘定を別々に管理する。

478 **投資銀行**は、通常、株式取引の手数料よりはむしろ顧客に請求する手数料で収益を得ている。

479 多くの銀行は、組織形態であるほうが単体の銀行であるよりもより収益性が高いと予測するため、自らを**銀行持株会社**に組織化している。

480 委託売買手数料の自由化は、**証券会社**間の価格競争を引き起こした。

481 **資産運用会社**は、主に顧客に課した資産管理手数料から収益を得ている。

482 Japan has "**non-bank** banks" - unregulated, non-deposit-taking institutions that borrow from regular banks at wholesale rates and lend the money out at retail rates.

483 In 2008, the federal government put both **Fannie Mae** and Freddie Mac into conservatorship because they were "de facto" bankrupt.

484 **Ginnie Mae** does not issue securities but rather guarantees securities issued by mortgage lenders.

485 In 2008, Iceland's three banks became bankrupt and were taken into **state ownership**, with huge international debts.

25 Interest Rates

486 Most **interest rates** are determined by the forces of supply and demand in the money or capital markets.

487 The demand for money is inversely related to the **nominal interest rate**.

488 If the inflation rate is higher than the nominal interest rate, then the **real interest rate** is negative.

482 日本には、**ノンバンク**が存在する。普通銀行から割引料金で借り入れ、リテールレートで貸し出す、規制の及ばない、預金の取扱いのない金融機関である。

483 2008年、連邦政府は、**ファニーメイ**と**フレディマック**が事実上の破綻に陥ったことから両社を政府管理下に置いた。

484 **ジニーメイ**は、証券を発行するのではなく、むしろ住宅ローン会社により発行された証券を保証する。

485 2008年、アイスランドの銀行が3行破綻のうえ、多額の対外債務を抱えたまま**国有化**された。

25　金　利

486 たいていの**金利**は、短期金融市場や資本市場における需給要因により決定される。

487 資金需要は、**名目金利**と逆向きの関係にある。

▶名目金利：物価上昇率などを加味しない表面上の金利

488 インフレ率が名目金利よりも高い場合、**実質金利**はマイナスになる。

▶実質金利：名目金利から物価変動の影響を除いた金利

489 The **yield curve** typically steepens in a bond market rally and flattens in a selloff.

490 The **positive yield** curve will be steepest when interest rates are expected to rise.

491 The idea that an **inverted yield** curve signals a forthcoming recession was formalized empirically by a number of researchers in the late 1980s.

492 In most currencies, **swap rates** are higher than government yields.

493 Most central banks in industrial countries have increasingly used **short-term interest rates** as the policy instrument or operating target.

494 In most currencies, there is usually a 10-year government bond rate that offers a reasonable measure of the **risk-free rate**.

495 To a large extent **long-term interest rates** are determined by bond prices and bond yields.

496 LIBOR is widely used as a benchmark interest rate for short-term floating-rate debt.

497 TIBOR became significantly higher than LIBOR during the period of the Japanese banking crisis.

489 **イールドカーブ**は一般に、債券相場の上昇時には急勾配になり（スティープ化）、下落時には平らになる（フラット化）。

▶ イールドカーブ：残存期間が異なる債券の利回りを描いた曲線

490 **順イールド**カーブは、金利の上昇が予測されるときに最も急勾配になる。

▶ 順イールド：イールドカーブが右上りの曲線になること

491 **逆イールド**カーブは景気後退の兆しを示すものであるという考えは、1980年代後期に多くの研究者によって経験的立証のもとに形成された。

▶ 逆イールド：イールドカーブが右下りの曲線になること

492 ほとんどの通貨では、**スワップレート**は国債の利回りよりも高い。

▶ スワップレート：金利スワップにおいてLIBORと固定金利を交換する際の固定金利

493 先進工業国でのほとんどの中央銀行は、**短期金利**を政策手段や操作目標としてますます利用するようになった。

494 ほとんどの通貨では、たいてい**無リスク金利**の適当な尺度となる10年物国債利率がある。

▶ 無リスク金利：リスクをもたない資産（安全資産）の期待リターン

495 大方の場合、**長期金利**は債券価格と債券利回りで決定される。

496 **LIBOR**（ロンドン銀行間取引金利）は短期変動金利債務に対しての基準金利として広く利用されている。

497 **TIBOR**（東京の銀行間取引金利）は、日本の金融危機の間、LIBORよりも著しく高くなった。

498 In November 1997, the **Japan premium** jumped to 90 basis points, reflecting the turmoil in the domestic money market.

499 Some economists believe that Japan was caught in a **liquidity trap** in the late 1990s.

26 Financial Regulation

500 Japanese banks and financial markets experienced a wave of **deregulation** and financial innovation during the 1980s.

501 The government implemented the **Financial System Reform** Law in 1992, which permitted banks, securities companies and trust banks to enter into each other's businesses.

502 The Financial Reform Law abolished in principle the **firewall** between banks and investment firms.

503 The Ministry of Finance in 1992 permitted banks to issue **subordinated debt** to meet BIS capital-asset requirements.

498 1997年11月、国内の短期金融市場の混乱を反映して、ジャパンプレミアムが90ベーシスポイントまで跳ね上がった。

▶ ジャパンプレミアム：日本の金融機関が海外の金融市場から資金調達するときに上乗せして要求される金利幅

499 経済学者のなかには、1990年代の終わり頃に、日本は流動性の罠にはまったと考える者がいる。

▶ 流動性の罠：利子率がゼロ近くまで下落すると投機的動機に基づく貨幣需要が無限大になる現象

26　金融規制

500 日本の銀行・金融市場は1980年代に、一連の規制緩和と金融制度革新を経験した。

501 政府は、1992年に金融制度改革法を実施し、これにより銀行、証券会社および信託銀行による相互参入が許可された。

502 金融制度改革法では、原則的には銀行と証券会社との間のファイアウォールを取り払った。

▶ ファイアウォール：金融機関などで部門間の交流を意図的に遮断すること

503 大蔵省（財務省）は1992年、BIS自己資本比率規制に対応するため、銀行が劣後債務を発行することを許可した。

▶ 劣後債務：破産・清算の際の返済順位が劣後する債務

504 The **Glass Steagall Act** was repealed in 1999 and financial establishments were permitted to offer both commercial and investment banking services.

505 The **Volcker Rule** bans proprietary trading by banking organizations and limits investments in hedge funds and private equity funds.

506 The so-called Volcker Rule was adopted by Congress in Section 619 of the **Dodd-Frank Act**.

507 The **Basel Standards** were adopted by the Basel Committee in 1988 for the purpose of creating common international capital adequacy standards.

508 In July 1988, it was decided that by the end of fiscal year 1991, banks should have a minimum **capital adequacy ratio** of 8%.

509 Under the Basel II rules, a weighting is assigned to each asset class to calculate the **risk-weighted assets**.

510 Banks should identify and assess the **operational risk** inherent in all products, activities, processes and systems.

511 The Basel III proposal sets a new **core Tier 1** ratio of 4.5% plus a new capital conservation buffer of a further 2.5%.

504 グラススティーガル法（米国）が1999年に無効となり、金融機関は、商業銀行業務および投資銀行業務の両方を提供することが許された。

505 ボルカールール（米国）では、銀行組織による自己勘定取引が禁止され、ヘッジファンドおよびプライベートエクイティファンドへの投資も制限している。

506 いわゆるボルカールールは、ドッドフランク法（米国）第619項で議会によって採択された。

507 国際的に共通の自己資本比率基準を創出する目的で、1988年にバーゼル基準がバーゼル委員会で採択された。

508 1991年度末までに銀行の最低自己資本比率は8％とするべしということが1988年7月に決定された。

▶ 自己資本比率《金融機関》：リスクアセットに対する自己資本の比率

509 バーゼルⅡ規制のもとでは、ウェイトが各資産クラスに割り当てられ、リスクアセットを算出する。

▶ リスクアセット：資産の種類ごとにウェイトを乗じて算出される、貸倒れリスクの総量

510 銀行は、すべての商品、活動、プロセスおよびシステムに内在するオペレーショナルリスクを特定し、評価すべきである。

▶ オペレーショナルリスク：事務ミス・システム障害・不正・法令違反・災害などに起因する損失

511 バーゼルⅢの提言では、4.5％の新しいコアTier1比率に加えて、さらに2.5％の新規資本保全バッファーが導入された。

▶ コアTier1：銀行の自己資本のうち中核的な部分（普通株と内部留保）

512 The Basel Committee on Banking Supervision proposed in 2009 two sets of standardized quantitative requirements to enhance **liquidity buffers** in the banking system.

513 The primary purpose of risk regulations is to prevent "**systemic risk**," or the risk of collapse of the entire system due to interconnections between financial firms.

514 Financial regulation is only one of the many tools that policy makers can use to mitigate **procyclicality**.

515 The current **solvency margin** ratios of major Japanese insurance companies stand above 700%, well in excess of the minimum 200% requirement.

516 Japan introduced a single **financial regulator** covering banking, securities, and insurance in June 1998.

27　Monetary Policy

517 Developed countries frequently designate price stability as the principal target of **monetary policy**.

512 バーゼル銀行監督委員会は2009年、金融制度における流動性バッファーの引上げのために必要な標準定量的要件を2点提案した。

▶ 流動性バッファー：金融機関が金融危機などの状況で追加的に充足できる現預金など

513 リスク規制の主要目的は、「システミックリスク」の防止、つまり金融会社間での相互関連性のゆえにシステム全体が崩壊するリスクを防止することである。

▶ システミックリスク：金融機関が連鎖的に決済不能となるリスク

514 金融規制は、景気循環増幅効果を緩和するために政策立案者たちが利用できる多くのツールの1つにすぎない。

▶ 景気循環増幅効果：金融規制が景気変動を増幅させてしまうこと

515 日本の主要保険会社の現在のソルベンシーマージン比率は700％を上回っており、200％という最低基準をはるかに超えている。

▶ ソルベンシーマージン：保険会社の保険金支払余力を測る指標

516 日本は、1998年6月、銀行業、証券、保険を対象とする単独の金融監督機関を導入した。

27 金融政策

517 先進諸国は物価安定を金融政策の主要目標として指定することが多い。

518 As with other developed countries, the main instrument for monetary policy in present Japan is the **open market operation**.

519 The BoJ's **buying operation** refers to its outright purchase of government bonds from the market to inject more liquidity into the banking system.

520 If the central bank conducts buying operations more frequently than **selling operations**, then monetary base is injected into the economy.

521 Since changing the **reserve requirement** is unable to produce subtle changes in the money supply, it is rarely used as a tool of monetary policy.

522 If the **reserve ratio** is raised, it means banks have to reduce their lending, so the money supply is reduced.

523 **Interest rate policy** is usually less effective in influencing domestic demand in emerging economies than in mature markets.

524 As a consequence of the **tight monetary policy**, the asset price bubble burst in the early 1990s.

518 他の先進諸国と同じく、現在の日本の金融政策の主要手段は、公開市場操作である。

> ▶ 公開市場操作：中央銀行が市場で有価証券を売買することで市中の通貨量を増減させる政策

519 日本銀行の買いオペとは、銀行業務システムにより多くの流動性を注入するための市場からの国債の買い切りを指す。

> ▶ 買いオペ：中央銀行が市場から有価証券を買い入れ、通貨を放出すること

520 中央銀行が売りオペよりも頻繁に買いオペを実施すれば、マネタリーベースが経済に投入される。

> ▶ 売りオペ：中央銀行が保有する有価証券を市場で売却し、通貨を回収すること

521 準備預金の変更では貨幣供給量の微妙な変化を生み出すことができないので、金融政策の手段としてはめったに用いられない。

> ▶ 準備預金：金融機関が中央銀行に預け入れる預金

522 支払準備率が上昇すると、銀行は貸出を減らさなくてはならないことになり、貨幣供給量も減少する。

> ▶ 支払準備率：金融機関が中央銀行へ預金を預ける割合

523 金利政策は通常、新興経済では、成熟市場におけるよりも国内需要への影響には効果が低い。

> ▶ 金利政策：中央銀行が景気が悪いときには金利を低くして金融緩和を行い、景気が過熱気味のときには金利を高くして金融引締めを行う政策

524 金融引締政策の結果、バブル景気は1990年の初め頃に崩壊した。

525 The Bank of Japan ran an excessively **accommodative monetary policy** for most of the 1980s.

526 The Bank of Japan employed **quantitative easing** from March 2001 to March 2006, yet the economy was in recession with deflation.

527 Between 1998 and 1999, the government of Japan made the **public fund** injection into private banks to strengthen the capital base twice.

528 Traditionally, central banks such as the Federal Reserve have provided a **discount window** facility to meet the short-term liquidity needs of banks.

529 The **Federal Open Market Committee** meets in Washington about eight times a year to decide how to implement monetary policy.

530 The **central banks** of most countries accept the need to act as lender of last resort for their domestic banking systems.

531 If the market interprets the **interest rate hike** as a sign of monetary tightening, the expectations effect will reinforce the interest rate hike.

532 The terrorist attacks in the United States led to a significant **interest rate cut** in September 2001.

525 日本銀行は、1980年代のほぼ全般に、過度の金融緩和政策を実施した。

526 日本銀行は、量的金融緩和を2001年の3月から2006年の3月まで採用したが、経済はデフレを伴う景気後退となった。
▶ 量的金融緩和：当座預金を金融調節の誘導目標とする政策

527 1998年から1999年の間に、日本政府は、銀行の自己資本を2倍に増強するために民間銀行に公的資金の注入をした。

528 従来、連邦準備銀行のような中央銀行は、銀行の手元流動性のニーズに応えるべく割引窓口貸出（ディスカウントウィンドウ）機能を提供してきた。
▶ 割引窓口貸出：中央銀行の民間金融機関向け常設貸出制度

529 FOMC（米国連邦公開市場委員会）は年に約8回ワシントンで会合し、金融政策の実施方法について決定する。

530 大多数の国の中央銀行は、国内の銀行制度に対しての最後の貸し手の役目を果たす必要性を認めている。

531 市場が利上げを金融引締めの兆候と判断すれば、その期待効果で金利上昇に拍車が掛かる。

532 米国でのテロ襲撃は、2001年9月、著しい利下げをもたらした。

533 In February 1999, the BOJ introduced an unprecedented **zero interest rate policy**, which lasted until August 2000.

534 In October 2008, major central banks across the world engaged in the biggest **coordinated interest rate cut** in the history.

535 Central banks typically announce a change in **key interest rates** which will then have knock-on effects down the whole interest rate structure.

536 The **Bank of Japan**'s two main missions are the implementation of monetary policy and the issuance and management of banknotes.

537 The **Federal Reserve Board** cut the federal funds rate to 0% to 0.25% in December 2008 from 5.25% in September 2007.

538 The **Bank of England** reduced interest rates steadily to 0.5% in March 2009.

539 The **European Central Bank** reduced interest rates sharply from late 2008 to historically low levels.

540 In 1990, the Bank of Japan raised the **official discount rate** to 6%.

541 The Bank of Japan lowered its **uncollateralized overnight call** rate marginally to 0.3% in October 2008 and further to 0.1% in December 2008.

533 1999年2月、日本銀行は前例のない**ゼロ金利政策**を導入し、2000年8月まで続いた。

534 2008年10月、世界中の大手中央銀行は、歴史上、最も大々的な**協調利下げ**に取り組んだ。

535 中央銀行は、概して、金利構造全体に波及効果を及ぼすような**政策金利**の変更を発表するものである。

536 **日本銀行**の2つの主な使命は、金融政策の実施と銀行券の発行と管理である。

537 **連邦準備制度理事会**は、フェデラルファンドレート（FFレート）を、2007年9月の5.25%から、2008年12月には0%～0.25%に引き下げた。

538 **イングランド銀行**は、2009年3月、金利を0.5%にまで着実に引き下げた。

539 **欧州中央銀行**は2008年後半から歴史的な低水準にまで金利を急激に引き下げた。

540 1990年、日本銀行は、**公定歩合**を6%まで引き上げた。
▶ 公定歩合：中央銀行の民間銀行への貸出基準金利

541 2008年10月、日本銀行は**無担保コール翌日物**金利をわずかに0.3%へ引き下げ、同年12月にはさらに0.1%まで引き下げた。

542 The **federal funds rate** rose from 1% in June 2004 to 5.25% beginning in June 2006.

543 The Bank of England raised its **repo rate** by a cumulative 150 basis points between May 1997 and June 1998, to 7.5%.

544 The **ECB interest rate** peaked at 4.75% in October 2000.

28 Securities Market

545 Global **securities markets** have become an increasingly important source of external funding for many emerging market countries.

546 The stocks of publicly traded companies are usually bought and sold on **stock exchanges**.

547 The vast majority of bond trading occurs in the **over-the-counter market**, directly between an investor and a bond dealer.

548 In many emerging markets trading is concentrated on a small proportion of **listed securities**.

549 **Unlisted securities** are harder to value than listed securities and are generally perceived to carry a greater degree of risk.

542 FFレート（フェデラルファンドレート）は、2004年6月の1％から2006年6月の初めには5.25％まで上がった。

543 イングランド銀行は、1997年5月から1998年6月の間にレポレートを7.5％まで、累計150ベーシスポイント引き上げた。

544 ECB政策金利は、2000年10月には4.75％というピークに達した。

28　証券市場

545 グローバル証券市場は、多くの新興市場の国々にとって、ますます重要な外部資金調達源となった。

546 上場会社の株は、たいてい証券取引所で売り買いされる。

547 債券取引の大部分は、店頭市場にて投資家と債券ディーラーとの間で直接行われる。

548 多くの新興市場では、取引は上場証券のごく一部に集中する。

549 非上場証券は上場証券よりも評価がむずかしく、一般的にはリスクも高いとみられている。

550 **Trading costs** include explicit commissions as well as the bid-ask spread.

551 In general, investors experience higher (or positive) returns on common stock investments during a **bull market**.

552 During **bear markets**, many investors choose vehicles other than securities to obtain higher and less risky returns.

553 Investors are prohibited from using **short selling** to protect themselves from falling security prices.

554 In Japan, all securities must be traded through an authorized securities **dealer** who is a member of the Japan Securities Dealers Association.

555 If the shares or debentures are not subscribed for by the public, the **underwriters** should take up the shares and pay for them.

556 In the wake of the stock market turmoil of 2008, **market regulators** all over the world started imposing restrictions on short selling.

557 In December 2005, the **market value** of the shares traded on the first section of the Tokyo Stock Exchange exceeded ¥500 trillion for the first time in 15 years.

550 取引コストには、ビッドアスクスプレッド（売値と買値の差）だけでなく明示的手数料も含まれる。

551 一般的に、投資家は、強気相場では普通株の投資でより高い（もしくはプラスの）リターンを経験する。

552 弱気相場では、多くの投資家は、より高く、よりリスクの低いリターンを得るために、証券以外のビークル（商品）を選択する。

553 投資家は、下落する証券価格から自らを守るための空売りの利用は禁止されている。

▶ 空売り：株式や債券などの現物を借りて売却すること

554 日本では、すべての証券は、日本証券業協会の会員である公認の証券ディーラー（会社）を経て取引しなくてはならない。

▶ ディーラー：証券の自己売買業務を行う者

555 株や債券が公開で引き受けられない場合は、アンダーライターが株を引き受け、その支払をしなければならない。

▶ アンダーライター：証券の引受業務を行う者

556 2008年の株式市場の大波乱の結果、世界中の市場規制当局が空売りについての規制を課し始めた。

557 2005年12月、東証一部で取引される株式の時価評価額は、15年ぶりに500兆円を超えた。

558 **Circuit breakers** give participants a chance to assess market fundamentals while prices are temporarily frozen.

559 **Basket trades** are popular among investors who are attempting to mimic a particular index.

560 **Trading limits** are designed to protect investors from wild price fluctuations and the potential for major losses.

561 **Insider trading** rules prohibit traders from attempting to profit from inside information.

562 **Market manipulation** is illegal in most countries except when it is done by the government or the central bank.

563 The Japanese anti-money laundering/counter-terrorist financing law requires the reporting of suspicious transactions in **money laundering** and terrorist financing cases.

29 Stocks

564 World **stock market** capitalization declined by 26,400 billion USD between July 2007 and November 2008.

558 **サーキットブレーカー**により価格が一時的に凍結されている間に、市場参加者はマーケットファンダメンタルズ(基礎的条件)を評価する機会が得られる。

▶ サーキットブレーカー:取引価格が一定の範囲を超えて変動した場合に、相場を安定させるため取引所が取引を一時中断すること

559 **バスケット取引**は、特定の指数に連動するような運用を試みる投資家達の間では好評である。

▶ バスケット取引:多数の銘柄をまとめて1つの商品として売買する取引

560 **値幅制限**は、株価の激変や巨大損失の可能性から投資家を保護するために考案されている。

561 **インサイダー取引**規制は、トレーダーが内部情報から利益を得ようとすることを禁止する。

562 **相場操縦**は、政府や中央銀行が実施する場合を除いて、ほとんどの国々では違法とされている。

563 日本のマネーロンダリング防止及びテロ資金対策法では、**マネーロンダリング**およびテロ資金調達において疑わしい取引は報告することが要求されている。

▶ マネーロンダリング:犯罪で得た不正資金を口座から口座へと転々とさせ、資金の出所や受益者を隠す行為

29　株　式

564 世界の**株式市場**の時価総額は2007年7月から2008年11月の間に、26兆4,000億米ドル減少した。

565 The **common stock** of most large corporations can be bought or sold freely on one or more stock exchanges.

566 Since **preferred stock** pays a fixed dividend, it is purchased primarily by investors who want a fixed flow of income.

567 Because many **large-cap stocks** are often considered much more secure than small-cap stocks, they may appeal to more conservative investors.

568 **Mid-cap stocks** provide much of the attraction of small-stock returns, without as much price volatility.

569 Since **small-cap stocks** are issued by smaller companies, they tend to be more speculative and are often purchased by speculators hoping to make a quick profit.

570 Most **cyclical stocks** are in basic industries such as automobiles, steel, paper, and heavy manufacturing.

571 **Defensive stocks** tend to be less affected than the average issue by downswings in the business cycle.

572 Stocks issued by electric, gas, telephone, and other utility companies are generally classified as **income stocks**.

573 People who invest in **blue-chip stocks** want some growth but primarily seek a safe investment.

565 ほとんどの大手企業の普通株は、単一もしくは複数の証券取引所で自由に売買できる。

566 優先株では固定の配当が支払われるので、安定した収益フローを望む投資家によって主に購入される。

▶ 優先株：配当金や残余財産を普通株よりも優先的に受け取ることができる株式

567 大型株の多くは、通常、小型株よりもはるかに安全であると考えられているため、より保守的な投資家向けであるかもしれない。

568 中型株では、さほど価格の変動もなく小型株のもつ魅力の多くを提供する。

569 小型株は小企業から発行されるため、より投機的傾向にあり、手っ取り早い利益を望む投機家に買われることが多い。

570 景気循環株のほとんどは、自動車、鉄鋼、製紙、重工業などの基幹産業の株である。

▶ 景気循環株：景気変動に伴い業績も変動する企業の株式

571 ディフェンシブ株は、平均銘柄よりも景気循環の下降局面による影響を受けにくい傾向にある。

▶ ディフェンシブ株：景気変動の影響を受けにくい企業の株式

572 電気、ガス、電話、その他公益事業会社によって発行された株は、一般的に資産株に分類される。

▶ 資産株：業績が安定しており長期保有に適した株式

573 優良株に投資する人々は、いくらかの増額も期待するも、本来は安全投資を求める人たちである。

574 Many corporations are reluctant to cut dividends because the corporation's **stock price** usually falls when a dividend reduction is announced.

575 The **equity premium** is very large, which means that the returns to stocks are dramatically higher than the returns to bonds.

576 International investors in general are not interested in **voting rights**.

577 Although **margin trading** can lead to increased returns, it also presents substantial risks.

578 **Nikkei 225** declined by 82% from its peak at 38,915 in December 1989 to its trough of 6,994 in October 2008.

579 **TOPIX** is a capitalization-weighted index of all companies listed on the first section of the Tokyo stock exchange.

580 Because the **DJIA** results from summing the prices of the 30 stocks, higher-priced stocks tend to affect the index more than do lower-priced stocks.

581 The **FTSE 100** peaked at 6,950.6 at the height of the dotcom boom in December 1999.

582 The **Nasdaq** stock index is heavily weighted with technology stocks.

574 減配を公表すると企業の株価はたいてい下落するので、多くの企業は減配をするのは控え気味である。

575 株式プレミアムは非常に大きく、これは、株式の収益率が債券の収益率よりも目覚ましく高いことを意味する。

▶ 株式プレミアム：株式投資のリターンのうち社債の利回りを上回る部分

576 外国人投資家は全般的に議決権には興味がない。

577 信用取引は利益の増額も見込めるが、相当なリスクも伴う。

▶ 信用取引：委託保証金を証券会社に担保として預託し、資金や証券を借りて売買を行う取引

578 日経平均株価は、ピーク時の1989年12月の38,915円から2008年10月の6,994円の底値まで82％下落した。

579 東証株価指数は、東証一部のすべての上場企業の時価総額加重平均型株価指数である。

580 ダウ平均株価（米国）は30種の株価の合計から算出されるため、値嵩株のほうが低位株よりも指数に影響を与える傾向がある。

581 FTSE100種総合株価指数（英国）は、1999年12月のITバブルの最盛期に、最高値6,950.6でピークに達した。

582 ナスダック株価指数（米国）は、テクノロジー関連株の比重が著しく高い。

583 The increase in **foreign share ownership** in Japan in the 1990s reflected a larger worldwide trend.

30　Bonds

584 Although the **bond market** is larger than the stock market, much of the activity within the bond market is generated by institutional investors rather than individual investors.

585 Japanese banks and financial institutions hold a large percentage of **government bonds**.

586 Markets normally perceive **municipal bonds** as implicitly guaranteed by the central government.

587 The creditworthiness of **government-guaranteed bonds** is assumed to be the same as that of government bonds.

588 Compared to government bonds, **corporate bonds** generally have a higher risk of default.

589 Bond issuance by the financial services sector has risen mainly since 1999 when commercial banks were allowed to issue **straight bonds**.

590 If the stock price falls, the **convertible bond**'s price drops less than the underlying stock.

583 1990年代の日本での外国人持株比率の上昇は、大きな世界的傾向を反映するものであった。

30　債　券

584 債券市場は株式市場よりも大きいが、債券市場内での動きの大部分は個人投資家ではなく機関投資家により生み出される。

585 日本の諸銀行と金融機関とで国債の大部分を保有している。

586 市場では、地方債は中央政府に暗黙のうちに保証されていると見込まれている。

587 政府保証債の信用力は、国債と同じと想定されている。

588 国債と比べて、社債は一般的に債務不履行のリスクが高い。

589 金融サービス部門による起債は、主に普通社債の発行が商業銀行に許可された1999年から増大した。

590 株価が下落すると、転換社債型新株予約権付社債の価格も下落するが、下げ幅は原株よりは小さい。

▶ 転換社債型新株予約権付社債：発行時に決められた価格で株式に転換することができる社債

591 The warrants which come attached to the **warrant bonds** can be detached and sold separately.

592 **Inflation-indexed bonds** are a financial innovation that disassociates two risks that had been intertwined: the coupon reinvestment risk and the inflation risk.

593 A bond linked to the Nikkei average is a **structured bond** that incorporates a Nikkei average option trading.

594 Private investors usually purchase **fixed-rate bonds** when they think that the interest rates will go down in the future.

595 **Floating-rate bonds** are beneficial vis-a-vis fixed-rate bonds to investors when interest rates are likely to rise.

596 **Zero coupon bonds** appreciate more than conventional fixed-income securities when interest rates decline.

597 The price of a **callable bond** is always lower and the yield higher than a straight bond.

591 ワラント債に付されたワラントは、切り離して別途売ることができる。

> ▶ ワラント債：発行会社の株式を決められた価格で買い付ける権利のついた社債

592 インフレ連動債は、クーポン再投資リスクとインフレリスクという2つの絡み合ってきたリスクを分離する金融革命である。

> ▶ インフレ連動債：元本や利息が物価指数に連動する債券

593 日経平均リンク債は、日経平均オプション取引が組み込まれた仕組債である。

> ▶ 仕組債：デリバティブが組み込まれ、特殊なキャッシュフローをもつ債券

594 個人投資家は、金利が将来下落すると思うと、固定利付債を購入する。

595 変動利付債は、利率が上がりそうな時期には、投資家にとって、固定利付債と比べて有利である。

596 ゼロクーポン債（割引債）は、金利が下がったときは、従来の確定利付証券よりも価値が上がる。

> ▶ zero coupon bond＝discount bond

597 コーラブル債の価格は普通社債よりも常に低くなり、利回りは高くなる。

> ▶ コーラブル債：債券の発行体が期限前償還できる条件が付された債券

598 A **puttable bond** protects investors from downside risk. Therefore, investors are willing to accept a lower yield when purchasing a puttable bond.

599 **Euroyen bond** market has grown substantially because of the liberal issue requirements.

600 In recent years many companies have been issuing **Samurai bonds** in Japan to take advantage of very low interest rates.

601 Fixed-rate interest payments on a **dual-currency bond** could be designated as the hedged transaction in a cash flow hedge of foreign exchange risk.

602 Many banks and other institutional investors are permitted by law to hold only **investment-grade bonds**.

603 **Junk bonds** are considered very high default risk and often require a premium of an additional 5% or more.

604 Although **secured bonds** might appear safer than unsecured bonds at first glance, this assumption may not be true.

598 プッタブル債は、値下りリスクから投資家を保護する。したがって、投資家は、プッタブル債を買う際には、低い利回りもあえて受け入れる。

▶ プッタブル債：債券の保有者が期限前償還を要求できる権利が付された債券

599 ユーロ円債市場は、発行条件が自由であることから、大きく成長した。

▶ ユーロ円債：発行通貨の自国市場以外の市場で発行される債券

600 近年、多くの企業が、非常に低い利率の利点を得るべく日本で円建て外債を発行している。

▶ 円建て外債：海外企業が日本国内で円建てで発行する債券

601 デュアルカレンシー債での固定金利の支払は、外国為替リスクのキャッシュフローヘッジにおけるヘッジ取引として指定されうる。

▶ デュアルカレンシー債：払込み・利払いと元本償還が別々の通貨建てで行われる債券

602 多くの銀行およびその他の機関投資家は法律によって、投資適格債のみ保有することが許可されている。

603 ジャンク債は不履行リスクが非常に高いと考えられており、5％以上の付加的プレミアムが要求されることがしばしばある。

▶ junk bond=high yield bond

▶ ジャンク債：投資不適格の格付を与えられた債券

604 一見、担保付債券は無担保債よりは安全であるようだが、その想定は必ずしも正しくはない。

605 Large corporations with good credit ratings use **unsecured bonds** extensively.

606 In general, the value of **short-term bonds** is far less volatile than that of long-term bonds, and thus short-term bonds are a safer investment.

607 With a barbell strategy, investments are only made in short-term and long-term bonds, not **intermediate-term bonds**.

608 Prices of **long-term bonds** are more sensitive to interest rate changes than prices of short-term bonds.

609 Most **super-long bonds** are sold through private placement to a few financial institutions.

610 The **coupon rate** is determined by the underlying strength of the company and the prevailing rates of interest in the marketplace.

611 The **yield to maturity** is greater than the coupon rate when the bond price is below its face value.

612 **Duration** is a measure of the sensitivity of a bond's price to interest rate movements.

613 When **bond prices** rise, interest rates will fall, and vice versa.

605 信用格付が良好な大手企業は、無担保債を広く利用する。

606 一般的に、短期債は、長期債よりもはるかに不安定さが少なく、したがって短期債はより安全な投資である。

607 バーベル戦略では、投資は短期債もしくは長期債のみになされ、中期債には投資されない。

608 長期債の価格は、短期債の価格よりも金利変動に敏感に反応しやすい。

609 超長期債のほとんどは、私募により少数の金融機関に対し売られている。

610 クーポン利率は、その企業の基礎的な強さと市場の現在の利子率により決定する。

611 最終利回りは、債券価格が額面を下回るときには、クーポン利率よりも高い。

612 デュレーションは、金利変動に対する債券価格の感度を示す尺度である。

▶ デュレーション：債券に投資された資金の平均回収期間

613 債券価格が上がると金利は下がり、またその逆も同様である。

614 When a bond series is issued, the issuer attempts to adjust its interest rate so that it can be sold at the **face value**.

615 A **yield spread** can apply to the differences in yield between any two or more types of securities, such as common stocks and bonds.

616 Most **JGBs** are held by domestic investors although the authorities have been marketing them actively to international investors in recent years.

617 In November 1998, interest rates on Japanese six-month **Treasury bills** turned slightly negative.

618 **Treasury notes** represent more than half of the negotiable debt issued by the government.

619 **Treasury bonds** have traditionally matured in 10 to 30 years and offer higher interest than Treasury notes.

620 **Gilts** are the main method by which the UK government finances the shortfall between its expenditure and its tax revenues.

621 The **bund** market is a large and liquid market and essentially the benchmark yield indicator for European government bonds.

614 一連の債券が発行されるとき、発行者は額面で売れるように利率の調整をしようとする。

615 利回り格差は、普通株と債券など2種類以上の証券の間での利回りの違いに相当する。

616 近年では、関係当局が外国人投資家に積極的に働きかけているが、日本国債（JGB）のほとんどは国内の投資家に保有されている。

617 1998年11月、日本の6カ月物短期国債の金利は、わずかにマイナスに転じた。

618 Tノート（米財務省中期債券）が、政府発行の譲渡可能債務の半分以上を占めている。

619 米長期国債は従来10〜30年で満期を迎え、Tノートよりも高額の利息をもたらす。

620 ギルト（英国債）は、英国政府が支出と税収入との間の不足分を調達する主たる手段である。

621 ブンズ（ドイツ国債）市場は大きく流動性のある市場で、基本的に、欧州諸国の国債にとってはベンチマークとなる利回り指標である。

622 **Mortgage bonds** are securities backed by a pool of mortgages, and the United States has the greatest mortgage securities market in the world.

623 The overall **Pfandbrief** market, with a volume outstanding of more than 1 trillion euros, is the biggest bond market within Europe.

31 Derivatives

624 The common reasons for using **financial derivatives** are: to hedge risks, to speculate or to lock in an arbitrage profit.

625 The **derivative securities** that are most widely held and traded include forward contracts, futures, options, and swaps.

626 **Forward contracts** are the most common means of hedging transactions in foreign currencies.

627 **Futures contracts** have standardized contract terms whereas the terms of forward contracts are individually negotiated.

628 A **swap** is an agreement between two counterparties to exchange future cash flows.

629 **Options** are a means for buyers to leverage the potential profits and limit the potential losses.

622 不動産抵当証券は、モーゲージプールにより裏付けされた証券で、米国は世界最大のモーゲージ証券市場を有する。

623 ファンドブリーフ市場全般は、１兆ユーロを超えるその規模から、欧州内では最大の債券市場である。

31　デリバティブ

624 デリバティブ（金融派生商品）を利用する一般的理由は、リスクを回避するため、投機目的、もしくは裁定利益を確定するためである。

625 最も広範囲にて保有され取引されているデリバティブ証券には、先渡契約、先物、オプション、スワップがある。

626 先渡契約は、外貨でのヘッジ取引の最も一般的な手段である。

627 先物契約には規格化された契約条件があるが、先渡契約の契約条件は個々に交渉される。

628 スワップとは、取引先同士の間での将来のキャッシュフローの交換についての契約のことである。

629 オプションとは、買い手が潜在的利益にレバレッジを効かせたり、また潜在的損失に制限を加えるための手段である。

630 **Interest rate futures** are inverted when the distant contracts are at a premium to near month contracts.

631 **Currency futures** are the same as forward exchange contracts, except that they trade on an exchange.

632 The **bond futures** price will be below spot prices if the yield curve is upward sloping.

633 An **interest rate swap** is especially useful for a company with a weak credit rating, since such entities must pay a premium to obtain fixed-rate debt.

634 The market for **currency swaps** comes primarily from corporations who can borrow in one currency at relatively favorable terms but need to borrow in another.

635 The most common type of a swap is the so-called **plain vanilla** interest rate swap.

636 The value of a **call option** increases when the price of the underlying security increases.

637 Profits on **put options** increase when the asset value falls.

630 金利先物取引では、期近物と比較して期先物のほうがプレミアムが高くなる場合に、逆転現象が生じる。

631 通貨先物取引は、取引所にて取引されるという点を除いては、先物為替予約と同じである。

632 イールドカーブが右上りであれば、債券先物価格は現物価格を下回るであろう。

633 金利スワップは、信用格付の低い企業にとっては特に有益である。そうした企業は、固定金利負債を得るのにプレミアムを払う必要があるからである。

634 通貨スワップの市場は、主に、比較的望ましい条件で1つの通貨で借入れができるが、別の通貨で借り入れる必要のある企業によって発生する。

635 スワップの最も一般的なタイプは、プレーンバニラ金利スワップである。

▶ プレーンバニラ：固定金利と変動金利の利息を交換する代表的な金利スワップ

636 原証券の価格が上昇すると、コールオプションの価値は増加する。

▶ コールオプション：オプション保有者が原資産を購入する権利

637 資産価値が下落すると、プットオプション取引の利益が増額する。

▶ プットオプション：オプション保有者が原資産を売却する権利

638 **Interest rate options** help investors to control the exposure to interest rate fluctuations and help the investors to take advantage of new investment opportunities.

639 A **currency option** is used at times of great uncertainty as insurance because it provides protection against adverse currency movements.

640 **Index options** do not require that the call writer actually "deliver the index" upon exercise or that the put writer "purchase the index."

641 The terms of **futures options** contracts are designed in effect to allow the option to be written on the futures price itself.

642 The buyer of a **swaption** has the right but not the obligation to enter into an interest rate swap agreement during the life of the option.

643 The main benefit of **credit derivatives** is to isolate the credit component of commonly traded instruments such as bonds and loans.

644 **Credit default swap** allows the creditor or the protection buyer to transfer credit risk to another party by paying a fixed amount.

638 **金利オプション**取引は投資家が金利変動リスクをコントロールするのに役立ち、また新規投資の機会をうまく利用するのにも役立つ。

639 **通貨オプション**は、不利な為替動向に対する防御になるため、非常に先行き不透明な時期には保険として利用される。

640 **指数オプション**では、コールオプションの売り手が、行使後すぐに実際に「インデックスを引き渡す」こと、もしくは、プットオプションの売り手が、「インデックスを購入する」ことを必要としない。

641 **先物オプション**の契約条件は、事実上、オプションが先物価格そのままに売りになるように考案されている。

642 **スワップション**の買い手には、オプションの権利行使可能期間に金利スワップ取引を交わす権利はあるが義務はない。

▶ スワップション：一定のスワップ取引を行う権利を売買するオプション取引

643 **クレジットデリバティブ**の主要な利点は、債券やローンなど、一般に取引される商品のクレジット要素を分離できることである。

▶ クレジットデリバティブ：企業の信用リスクを対象としたデリバティブ

644 **クレジットデフォルトスワップ（CDS）**では、債権者もしくはプロテクションの買い手がある固定額を支払うことによって別の当事者に信用リスクを転移することができる。

▶ クレジットデフォルトスワップ（CDS）：企業の債務不履行に伴うリスクを対象としたデリバティブ

645 The **contract for difference** requires payment of the difference between the current price and the price at some future date.

646 Individual investors seeking new investment opportunities supported the expansion in **foreign exchange margin trading**.

647 The most prevalent use of **weather derivatives** has been to hedge uncertainty in volumetric demand for energy, due to temperature fluctuations.

32 Investment Trusts

648 In June 2000, net assets of publicly offered **investment trusts** exceeded 60 trillion yen, an all-time high.

649 The Japanese tax laws define **stock investment trusts** as funds that hold even a small number of stocks.

650 **Bond investment trusts** are funds that invest not in stocks but only in bonds.

645 差金決済取引では、現在の価格と将来のある日付における価格との差額を支払う必要がある。

> ▶差金決済取引：原資産となる株価や指数を参照して差金決済による通貨の売買を行う取引

646 新たに投資の機会を探す個人投資家たちが、外国為替証拠金取引の拡張を支えた。

> ▶外国為替証拠金取引：保証金を業者に預託し、主に差金決済による通貨の売買を行う取引

647 天候デリバティブの利用で、これまでに最も浸透しているのは、気温の変動ゆえのエネルギー需要測定における不確実性を回避するための利用である。

> ▶天候デリバティブ：気象現象によって発生するリスクを対象としたデリバティブ

32　投資信託

648 2000年6月に、公募投資信託の純資産は60兆円を超え、史上最高となった。

649 日本の税法では、株式投資信託を、少数でも株式を保有するファンドと定義する。

650 債券投資信託は、株式には投資せず債券のみに投資するファンドである。

651 Investment in an **index fund** is a low-cost way for small investors to pursue a passive investment strategy.

652 **Balanced funds** offer the benefits of diversification in a single investment — with the accompanying risks of each asset class the funds hold.

653 **Open-end funds** continuously accept new money, and thus issue additional shares.

654 Since **closed-end funds** do not need to maintain cash reserves or sell securities to meet redemptions, they have the flexibility to invest in less liquid securities.

655 The **sector fund** concept is based on the belief that the really attractive returns come from small segments of the market.

656 More than 80 million people, or half of the households in the United States, invest in **mutual funds**.

651 **インデックスファンド**への投資は、小口投資家にとっては、パッシブ運用戦略を実施するのに低コストな方法である。

▶ インデックスファンド：基準価額が特定の指標（インデックス）と同じ値動きを目指す投資信託

652 **バランスファンド**は単一商品への投資により分散投資できる利点があるが、ファンドが抱える各資産クラスのリスクも伴う。

▶ バランスファンド：株式や債券など異なる資産が組み合わされた投資信託

653 **オープンエンド型ファンド**は、継続的に新規資金を受け付け、追加で証券を発行する。

▶ オープンエンド型ファンド：販売会社を通じて、原則としていつでも中途解約できる投資信託

654 **クローズドエンド型ファンド**は、支払備金を保持したり、買戻しに対応するために証券を売ったりする必要がないため、流動性の低い証券に投資する柔軟性がある。

▶ クローズドエンド型ファンド：原則として中途解約できない（上場されていれば取引所を通じて売却できる）投資信託

655 **セクターファンド**のコンセプトは、真に魅力的な利益は市場の小さな部分から得られるものであるという考えに基づいている。

▶ セクターファンド：特定の業種のみに投資する株式投資信託

656 8,000万人を超える人々、もしくは米国の世帯の半分は、**ミューチュアルファンド**に投資している。

▶ ミューチュアルファンド：米国のオープンエンド型の投資信託

657 One of the advantages of **separately managed accounts** is improved tax management.

658 **Exchange traded funds** offer investors relatively low trading costs and management fees, diversification, liquidity and tax efficiency.

659 The manager of a **fund of funds** pools capital from investors and then allocates it to two or more hedge fund managers.

660 **Growth funds** invest principally in well-established, large- or mid-cap companies that have above-average growth potential.

661 **Value funds** confine their investing to stocks considered to be undervalued by the market.

662 **Real estate investment trusts** give small investors the profit opportunities and advantages that come from large-scale real estate ownership.

663 In September 2001, the first Japanese-style real estate investment trust (**J-REIT**) was listed on a securities exchange market.

664 **Money management funds** specialize in investing in short-term instruments, which makes them very liquid.

665 **Money market funds** are aimed at protecting capital and offering a high income at the same time.

657 SMA（ラップ口座）の利点の１つは、税務管理が向上することである。

▶ SMA（ラップ口座）：顧客がファンドマネージャーに投資を委託する一任勘定口座

658 ETF（上場投資信託）は、投資家にとって取引費用や管理費が比較的安く、分散投資効果や流動性、節税効果ももたらす。

▶ ETF（上場投資信託）：証券取引所に上場され取引される投資信託

659 ファンドオブファンズのマネージャーは投資家から資金を集め、複数のヘッジファンドマネージャーに配分する。

▶ ファンドオブファンズ：他の複数の投資信託に投資する投資信託

660 成長株ファンドでは、主として、潜在的に平均以上の成長性が見込まれる安定した大型株もしくは中型株の会社に投資される。

661 割安株ファンドは、市場では割安と考えられている株を対象とした投資に限定する。

662 不動産投資信託は、小口投資家に、大型不動産の保有から見込める利益獲得機会と利点をもたらす。

663 2001年９月、初めてのJ-REIT（日本型不動産投資信託）が、証券取引市場に上場された。

664 MMF（マネーマネージメントファンド）は、短期商品への投資に特化しているため、非常に流動性が高い。

▶ MMF（マネーマネージメントファンド）：安全性の高い公社債などで運用される投資信託の一種

665（米国の）MMF（マネーマーケットファンド）は、元本の保護とともに高利回りの提供を目指している。

33 Investment Funds

666 **Hedge funds** are also called absolute return strategies because their goal is to produce positive return regardless of market direction.

667 **Buyout funds** invest in mature companies with historical track records and established management teams.

668 A **venture capital fund** is essentially invested in equity shares or equity-linked instruments of unlisted companies.

669 Institutional investors conduct extensive due diligence in order to assess prospective performance of a new **private equity fund.**

33 投資ファンド

666 **ヘッジファンド**は、市場動向に関係なく、プラスのリターンを生み出すのが目的であるため、絶対リターン戦略とも呼ばれている。

▶ヘッジファンド：金融派生商品などを活用してさまざまな手法で運用するファンド

667 **バイアウトファンド**は、過去実績があり、確立された経営陣が存在する成熟した企業に投資する。

▶バイアウトファンド：企業の株式を買収し、その企業価値を高めて売却することで利益を得るファンド

668 **ベンチャーキャピタルファンド**は、元来非上場企業の普通株もしくは株式関連商品に投資される。

▶ベンチャーキャピタルファンド：主に高い成長率をもつ未上場企業に投資して利益を得るファンド

669 機関投資家は、新規**プライベートエクイティファンド**の見込み収益を評価するべく広範囲にわたってデューデリジェンスを実施する。

▶プライベートエクイティファンド：未公開株式や事業に投資し、企業の成長や再生の支援を行うことで企業価値を高めて売却することで利益を得るファンド

670 Oil is a major source of capital for a majority of **sovereign wealth funds**.

671 **Managed futures** strategies, also known as 'CTA' strategies, seek returns through taking long and short positions in the global futures markets.

672 **Long/short fund** managers tend to focus on a particular type of stock, like small-cap stocks, or particular sectors.

673 **Market neutral** strategies are designed to eliminate systematic risk factors such as stock market or interest rate risk.

674 **Market timing** is commonly defined as being either fully invested in the market or fully invested in cash.

670 石油は大半のソブリンウェルスファンドにとっての主要財源である。

▶ ソブリンウェルスファンド：政府や中央銀行など国営機関が運用するファンド

671 CTA 戦略としても知られているマネージドフューチャーズ戦略は、世界中の先物市場においてロングポジションやショートポジションをとることで利益を追求する。

▶ マネージドフューチャーズ：株式・債券から原油・貴金属・農産物などの商品までさまざまな投資対象に投資するファンド

672 ロングショートファンドのマネージャーは、小型株のような特定の種類の株式または特定業種に集中する傾向にある。

▶ ロングショートファンド：値上りが期待できる銘柄を買い、同時に値下りが予想される銘柄を空売りするファンド

673 マーケットニュートラル戦略は、株式市場リスクや金利リスクのようなシステマティックリスク要因を排除するように考案されている。

▶ マーケットニュートラル：売りと買いを組み合わせることで市場の影響を受けない安定的な収益を目指す投資手法

674 マーケットタイミングは、一般的には、100％株式市場に投資するか、それとも現金で保有するか（市場の頃合を見定めること）であると定義される。

▶ マーケットタイミング：市場動向等を見計らい、安値で購入し高値で売却することを目的とする投資手法

675 **Event-driven funds** seek to exploit pricing inefficiencies created by actual or anticipated corporate events such as mergers or acquisitions.

34　Portfolio Investment

676 Inefficient or weakly efficient markets suggest that investors may be able to earn returns in excess of the markets by pursuing **active investment** strategies.

677 Under a pure **passive investment** strategy, an investor holds a portfolio that is an exact copy of the market index.

678 Studies have shown that as much as 90% or more of a portfolio's return comes from **asset allocation**.

679 An investor can reduce risk through a **diversified investment** portfolio.

680 There is a growing trend for big institutional investors to allocate larger proportions of their investment portfolios to **alternative investment** funds.

675 **イベントドリブンファンド**は、合併もしくは買収などのような、実際に企業に起こったイベントもしくは予測されるイベントによって発生した価格設定の非効率性を活用しようと努める。

▶ イベントドリブンファンド：M&A などのイベント発生時における市場のミスプライスを収益機会ととらえる投資手法

34　証券投資

676 非効率的もしくは弱度効率的市場は、投資家達が**アクティブ運用**戦略を実行することで市場を上回るリターンを得ることができるかもしれないということを示唆している。

▶ アクティブ運用：市場の平均を超えるリターンを追求する運用スタイル

677 まったくの**パッシブ運用**戦略下では、投資家は、市場指数の正確なコピーであるポートフォリオを保有している。

▶ パッシブ運用：市場平均と連動した運用成果を目標とする運用スタイル

678 ポートフォリオの収益の90％以上は**資産配分**からもたらされるということが研究で示された。

679 投資家は、**分散投資**ポートフォリオによりリスクを軽減することができる。

680 大手機関投資家たちが自身の投資ポートフォリオを、**オルタナティブ投資**ファンドに多めの比率で割り振る傾向がふえつつある。

▶ オルタナティブ投資：株式や債券など伝統的な資産とは異なる資産への投資

681 80 to 90% of global **equity investment** originates and is invested in the developed markets of Europe, the United States, Canada, and Japan.

682 **Fundamental analysis** determines whether the price of a common stock reflects its intrinsic value.

683 Most foreign investors are **institutional investors** managing large pension funds, investment funds, and hedge funds.

684 The spread of personal computers and the Internet boosted the number of **individual investors**.

685 If the futures price deviates from fair value, it may be possible to construct an index **arbitrage trade**.

686 Foreign exchange trading exceeds a trillion dollars a day, though much of that total is **speculative trading**.

687 While Japanese households prefer assets that guarantee **principal**, their American counterparts prefer investment performance.

688 **Profit taking** sometimes causes a temporary market downturn after a period of rising prices.

689 Investors should decide on the basis of a trade-off between risk and **expected return**.

681 全世界の株式投資の80〜90％は、欧州や米国、カナダ、日本の先進国市場に生じ、またこれらの市場に投資されている。

682 ファンダメンタル分析で、普通株の価格がその内在価値を反映しているか否かがわかる。

> ▶ ファンダメンタル分析：景気や国際環境などの外部環境や企業の財務体質・業績についての分析

683 大多数の外国人投資家は、大規模な年金基金、投資ファンドおよびヘッジファンドを運用している機関投資家である。

684 パソコンとインターネットの普及で、個人投資家の数がふえた。

685 先物価格が公正価格から逸脱している場合には、指数裁定取引を構築できる可能性がある。

686 外国為替取引は1日で1兆ドルを超えるが、そのほとんどは投機取引である。

687 日本の家計は元本を保証する資産志向であるが、米国では運用実績志向である。

688 利食いによって、時折、物価上昇の期間の後に一時的な市場の冷え込みが生じる。

689 投資家は、リスクと期待リターンとのトレードオフに基づいて意思決定すべきである。

690 A large corporation may be thought to have a relatively low default risk and hence carry a low **risk premium**.

691 It is generally thought that **risk tolerance** decreases with age, although this relationship may not necessarily be linear.

692 Hedge funds might be exposed to a huge **downside risk** that is not easily detected by traditional risk measures.

693 The "**flight to quality**" occurs when capital is moved from risky to safe investments.

694 Fund managers are legally required to state in their advertisements that "past **investment performance** is no guarantee of future results."

695 The average **rate of return** on stocks of high-risk firms is much higher than the average rate of return of stocks of low-risk firms.

696 Low dividend firms presumably offer greater prospects for **capital gains**, or investors would not be willing to hold these stocks in their portfolios.

690 大手企業は不履行リスクが比較的低いと思われ、ゆえにリスクプレミアムは低い。

▶ リスクプレミアム：リスクの高い投資に対して投資家がそのリスク分に対して要求する超過収益

691 リスク許容度は年齢を重ねるにつれて低くなると一般的に考えられているが、この関係は必ずしも直線的ではない。

692 ヘッジファンドは、従来のリスク尺度では簡単に検出できない巨大な下方リスクにさらされる可能性がある。

693 「質への逃避」は、資本が危険な投資から安全な投資へと移動する際に生じる。

▶ 質への逃避：金融市場の先行きへの不安感が高まったときに、投資対象が相対的にリスクが低い資産へ動くこと

694 ファンドマネージャーは「過去の運用実績は将来の成果を保証するものではない」と、自らの広告に明言することを法的に求められる。

695 高リスクを伴う会社の株式の平均収益率は、低リスクを伴う会社の株式の平均利益率よりもはるかに高い。

696 配当金の少ない会社はキャピタルゲインに対し多めの見通しを示すであろう。そうでもしなければ、投資家はこのような株式を自らのポートフォリオにあえて保有しようとはしないであろう。

▶ キャピタルゲイン：保有資産の価格が上昇することによる収益

697 If the investor has a **capital loss** after subtracting capital gains, that net capital loss is used to offset income from other sources, such as dividends or interest.

698 The **time-weighted rate of return** enables a fund manager to be evaluated separately from the movements of capital.

699 An important idea in modern portfolio theory is for a manager to maximize **excess returns** relative to the excess risk.

700 The higher the **Sharpe ratio**, the better the historical risk-adjusted performance.

697 キャピタルゲインを差し引いた後に**キャピタルロス**が投資家にあれば、その純キャピタルロスは、配当や利息など他の収益源からの収益を相殺するのに使われる。

▶ キャピタルロス：保有資産の価格が下落することによる損失

698 **時間加重収益率**でファンドマネージャーを元本移動とは切り離して評価することができる。

▶ 時間加重収益率：運用者が自ら決めることができない運用元本の流出入の影響を排除して算出した収益率

699 近代ポートフォリオ理論において重要とされる考え方は、マネージャーが超過リスクに比して**超過収益**を最大化することである。

700 **シャープレシオ**が高ければ高いほど、過去のリスク調整後実績が良好である。

▶ シャープレシオ：（リターン－無リスク資産のリターン）÷リターンの標準偏差

【引用文献】

複数の引用を行った代表的な書籍・雑誌のみを掲載しています。

Wall Street Journal
Accounting, Carl S. Warren, James M. Reeve, Jonathan E. Duchac
Accounting Best Practices, Steven M. Bragg
Accounting: Tools for Business Decision Making, Paul D. Kimmel, Jerry J. Weygandt, Donald E. Kieso
All About Bonds and Bond Mutual Funds, Esme E. Faerber
An Introduction to Capital Markets, Andrew Chisholm
An Introduction to Investment Banks, Hedge Funds, and Private Equity, David Stowell
Annual Report on the Japanese Economy and Public Finance, Naikakufu
Bank of Japan Monetary and Economic Studies, Nihon Ginkō. Kinyū Kenkyūkyoku
Bonds: An Introduction to the Core Concepts, Mark Mobius
Business, William M. Pride, Robert J. Hughes, Jack R. Kapoor
Corporate Finance, Jonathan Berk, Peter DeMarzo
Corporate Finance Fundamentals, Stephen A. Ross, Randolph W. Westerfield, Bradford D. Jordan
Corporate Finance: Theory and Practice, Pascal Quiry, Yann Le Fur, Antonio Salvi
Economic and Social Survey of Asia and the Pacific, United Nations
Economic Survey of Japan, Japan. Keizai Kikakuchō
Essentials of Investments, Zvi Bodie, Alex Kane, Alan J. Marcus
Exchange Rate, Monetary and Financial Issues and Policies In Asia, Ramkishen S. Rajan, Shandre Thangavelu, Rasyad A. Parinduri
Financial Accounting, Jerry J. Weygandt, Paul D. Kimmel, Donald E. Kieso
Financial Accounting Theory, William R. Scott
Financial Management, Jae K. Shim, Joel G. Siegel
Financial Markets and Institutions, Frederic S. Mishkin, Stanley G.

Eakins
Financial Markets and Institutions, Jeff Madura
Fundamentals of Financial Management, Banerjee Bhabatosh
Fundamentals of Investing, Lawrence J. Gitman, Michael D. Joehnk
Guide to Economic Indicators, The Economist
Guide to Financial Markets, Marc Levinson
Guide to Japanese Taxes, Yūji Gomi
Handbook of Finance: Financial Markets and Instruments, Frank J. Fabozzi
International Economic Indicators and Central Banks, Anne Dolganos Picker
International Finance, Ephraim Clark
International Financial Management, Thummuluri Siddaiah
International Monetary and Financial Economics, Joseph P. Daniels, David D. VanHoose
Introduction to Corporate Finance, William L. Megginson, Scott B. Smart
Introduction to Finance: Markets, Investments, and Financial Management, Ronald W. Melicher, Edgar A. Norton
Investment Analysis, Chandra
Japanese Financial Markets, Junichi Ujiie
Japanese Investment in the World Economy, Roger Farrell
Japanese Management Accounting Today, Yasuhiro Monden, Masanobu Kosuga
Japan's Economic Revival: Policy Challenges in a Globalized World, Daniel Citrin
Japan's Financial Crisis: Institutional Rigidity and Reluctant Change, Jennifer Ann Amyx
Journal of the Japanese and International Economies, Tōkyō Keizai Kenkyū Sentā
Macroeconomics, Edward Gamber, David C Colander
Macroeconomics, Errol D'Souza
Macroeconomics, N. Gregory Mankiw
Macroeconomics, William Boyes, Michael Melvin

Macroeconomics: Principles & Policy, William J. Baumol, Alan S. Blinder
Managing Investment Portfolios: A Dynamic Process, John L. Maginn, Donald L. Tuttle, Dennis W. McLeavey
Mergers, Acquisitions, and Corporate Restructurings, Patrick A. Gaughan
Money and Banking: A Policy-oriented Approach, Dean Croushore
Money, Banking, and the Financial System, R. Glenn P. Hubbard, Anthony P. O'Brien
Money, the Financial System, and the Economy, R. Glenn Hubbard
Multinational Finance, Kirt Butler
OECD Economic Surveys, OECD
Personal Finance, Jack R. Kapoor, Les R. Dlabay, Robert J. Hughes
Personal Financial Planning, Lewis J. Altfest
Principles of Corporate Finance, Richard A. Brealey, Stewart C. Myers, Franklin Allen
Principles of Economics, John B. Taylor, Akila Weerapana
Securities Market in Japan, Japan Securities Research Institute
Standard & Poor's Creditweek, Standard and Poor's Corporation
Standard & Poor's Dictionary of Financial Terms, Virginia B. Morris, Kenneth M. Morris
The Business of Investment Banking: A Comprehensive Overview, K. Thomas Liaw
The Complete Guide to Investing During Retirement, Thomas Maskell
The Japanese Banking Crisis of the 1990s, Akihiro Kanaya, D. Woo
The Japanese Economy, David Flath
Understanding Financial Statements, Lyn M. Fraser
World Economic Outlook, International Monetary Fund

索 引（英文） ※数字はセンテンスの番号

A

accommodative monetary policy	525
accounting for income taxes	281
accounts payable	244
accounts receivable	238
acid-test ratio	287
acquisition	411
acquisition cost	272
active investment	676
additional paid-in capital	247
adjustable-rate mortgage	170
affiliated company	278
alternative investment	680
appreciation of the yen	124
arbitrage trade	685
Asian financial crisis	6
asset	232
asset acquisition	412
asset allocation	678
asset management company	481
asset value inflation	55
asset-backed commercial paper	387
asset-backed securities	385
asset-based lending	386
Australian dollar	143
automobile industry	442
automobile insurance	193

B

balance of payment	68
balance of trade	70
balance sheet	229
balanced fund	652
bank holding company	479
bank loan	350
Bank of England	538
Bank of Japan	536
banking system	351
Basel standard	507
basket trade	559
bear market	552
Black Monday	2
blue-chip stock	573
bond futures	632
bond investment trust	650
bond market	584
bond price	613
book value	271
book value per share	309
Brazilian real	144
break-even point	303
Bretton Woods System	116
BRICs	84
bubble economy	3
budget deficit	198
budget surplus	197
bull market	551
bund	621
business cycle	34
business investment	20
buying operation	519
buyout fund	667

C

call option	636
callable bond	597
Canadian dollar	142
capacity utilization rate	302

capital account	72	consolidated financial statement	275
capital adequacy ratio	508	consolidation	409
capital expenditure	319	construction industry	445
capital gain	696	consumer confidence index	37
capital goods	98	consumer electronics industry	444
capital increase	325	consumer finance	175
capital inflow	78	consumer goods	99
capital loss	697	consumer price index	47
capital market	454	consumer spending	16
capital outflow	79	consumption tax	221
capital stock	246	contract for difference	645
carry trade	112	contractionary fiscal policy	211
cash dividend	334	convertible bond	590
cash equivalent	236	coordinated intervention	121
cash flow	260	coordinated interest rate cut	534
central bank	530	core tier one	511
checking account	459	corporate bond	588
chemical industry	437	corporate bond spread	371
circuit breaker	558	corporate goods price index	48
clean surplus	285	corporate governance	396
closed-end fund	654	corporate income tax	220
collateral	354	corporate pension	397
collateralized bond obligation	390	corporate restructuring	427
collateralized debt obligation	388	cost inflation	54
collateralized loan obligation	389	cost of capital	313
collateralized mortgage obligation	391	cost of debt	314
commercial bank	475	cost of equity	315
commercial mortgage-backed securities	394	cost of goods sold	250
commercial paper	461	counterparty risk	372
commercial property	179	country risk	470
commitment line	359	coupon rate	610
commodity price	64	credit card	176
common stock	565	credit crunch	363
comprehensive income	270	credit default swap	644
conglomerate	415	credit derivative	643
		credit rating	374

credit risk	369
credit spread	370
creditor nation	73
cross-shareholdings	346
crowding-out	212
crude oil price	65
currency crisis	135
currency devaluation	129
currency fluctuation	128
currency futures	631
currency option	639
currency swap	634
currency swap arrangement	136
currency trading	127
current account	69
current asset	235
current liability	242
current ratio	286
cyclical stock	570

D

dealer	554
debit card	177
debt financing	320
debt for equity swap	347
debt to equity ratio	289
debtor nation	74
debtor-in-possession financing	343
debt-servicing cost	204
defensive stock	571
deferred tax asset	282
defined benefit	398
defined contribution	399
deflation	62
deflationary spiral	63
deposit insurance	165
depreciation	253

depreciation of the dollar	125
depression	32
deregulation	500
derivative securities	625
diffusion index	36
direct financing	322
direct investment	77
direct tax	217
discount window	528
discretionary fiscal policy	209
disinflation	61
disposable income	157
diversified investment	679
dividend payout ratio	336
dividend yield	335
DJIA	580
Dodd-Frank Act	506
dollar peg	133
domestic demand	24
dot com bubble	7
double taxation	226
downside risk	692
dual currency bond	601
duration	612

E

earnings announcement	267
earnings forecast	266
earnings per share	308
EBITDA	259
ECB interest rate	544
economic expansion	29
economic growth	26
economic indicator	35
economic recovery	28
economic slowdown	30
effective exchange rate	106

electric power industry	447
electrical and electronics industry	443
emerging market	83
employees' pension	188
employment insurance	185
enterprise value	312
equity financing	321
equity investment	681
equity premium	575
equity ratio	288
ESOP	402
euro	148
Eurocurrency	153
Eurodollar	154
Euromarket	155
European Central Bank	539
European debt crisis	11
European Monetary System	150
European Monetary Union	151
euroyen bond	599
event-driven fund	675
excess return	699
exchange intervention	120
exchange rate	104
exchange rate forecast	110
exchange traded fund	658
expansionary fiscal policy	210
expected return	689
export dependence	90
external debt	75
external rating	375

F

face value	614
factoring	384
fair value	273
Fannie Mae	483
federal funds rate	542
Federal Open Market Committee	529
Federal Reserve Board	537
financial account	71
financial asset	159
financial crisis	10
financial deficit	465
financial derivative	624
financial institution	474
financial lease	284
financial liberalization	467
financial market	452
financial regulator	516
financial risk	291
financial statement	228
financial surplus	464
Financial System Reform	501
financing cash flow	264
firewall	502
fiscal policy	208
fixed assets tax	222
fixed cost	305
fixed exchange rate system	117
fixed-rate bond	594
fixed-rate mortgage	169
flight to quality	693
floating exchange rate system	118
floating-rate bond	595
food industry	435
foreign currency	130
foreign currency reserve	76
foreign demand	25
foreign exchange hedging	109
foreign exchange margin trading	646

foreign exchange market	103
foreign exchange risk	108
foreign exchange trading	107
foreign share ownership	583
foreign trade	87
forward contract	626
free cash flow	261
free trade	101
friendly acquisition	422
FTSE 100	581
fund of funds	659
fundamental analysis	682
futures contract	627
futures option	641

G

GDP deflator	50
GDP growth	22
gift tax	224
gilt	620
Ginnie Mae	484
Glass Steagall Act	504
gold price	66
gold standard	115
golden share	426
goodwill	280
government bond	585
government expenditure	200
government revenue	199
government spending	18
government-guaranteed bond	587
Great Depression	1
gross domestic product	12
gross profit	251
gross profit margin	297
group insurance	195
growth fund	660

H

hedge against inflation	57
hedge fund	666
holding company	416
Hong Kong dollar	139
horizontal integration	420
horizontal merger	413
hostile takeover	423
housing permit	41
housing price	180
housing start	40
hybrid securities	348
hyperinflation	60

I

impairment loss	274
import dependence	91
income inequality	158
income statement	230
income stock	572
index fund	651
index option	640
indirect financing	323
indirect tax	218
individual income tax	219
individual investor	684
industrial production	38
inflation	52
inflation pressure	56
inflation rate	53
inflation targeting	58
inflation-indexed bond	592
inheritance tax	223
initial public offering	328
insider trading	561
institutional investor	683
insurance company	190

intangible asset	241
interbank market	462
interest coverage ratio	294
interest rate	486
interest rate cut	532
interest rate futures	630
interest rate hike	531
interest rate option	638
interest rate policy	523
interest rate risk	469
interest rate swap	633
interest-bearing liabilities	293
intermediate-term bond	607
internal rate of return	318
International Financial Reporting Standards	268
International Monetary Fund	80
international monetary system	114
inventory	239
inventory investment	21
inverted yield	491
investing cash flow	263
investment bank	478
investment banking	367
investment grade	378
investment grade bond	602
investment performance	694
investment spending	17
investment trust	648
Islamic finance	85

J

Japan premium	498
Japanese yen	137
J-curve	126
JGB	616
jobless claim	44
jobless recovery	8
joint venture	429
J-REIT	663
junk bond	603

K

key currency	131
key interest rate	535

L

labor productivity	300
labor share	301
land price	181
large-cap stock	567
leverage ratio	290
leveraged buyout	432
liability	233
liability-driven investment	400
LIBOR	496
life insurance	191
lifetime employment	403
like for like sales	42
line of credit	361
liquidity buffer	512
liquidity risk	472
liquidity trap	499
listed securities	548
living expense	160
loan business	349
loan on bills	356
loan on deeds	355
local government finance	207
local tax	216
long/short fund	672
long-term bond	608
long-term interest rate	495
lost decade	4

M

machinery industry	441
machinery order	39
main bank	341
managed futures	671
management buyout	431
manufacturing industry	434
margin trading	577
marginal cost	307
marginal revenue	306
market manipulation	562
market neutral	673
market regulator	556
market risk	468
market timing	674
market value	557
medical expense	161
medical insurance	183
mergers and acquisitions	407
mezzanine finance	383
mid-cap stock	568
military spending	206
minimum capital requirement	324
minimum wage	404
minority interest	279
monetary base	458
monetary policy	517
money laundering	563
money management fund	664
money market	453
money market fund	665
money stock	457
mortgage bond	622
mortgage-backed securities	392
municipal bond	586
mutual fund	656

N

Nasdaq	582
national income	156
national pension	187
national tax	215
negative net worth	292
negotiable certificate of deposit	460
net income	258
net present value	317
new economy	5
Nikkei 225	578
nominal GDP	14
nominal interest rate	487
non-bank	482
non-current liability	245
nonfarm payroll	45
non-operating expense	256
non-operating income	255
nonperforming loan	362
nonrecourse loan	172
non-tariff barrier	95
notes payable	243
notes receivable	237
nursing insurance	184

O

offer for sale	333
official discount rate	540
offshore currency trading	134
offshore market	466
open economy	100
open market	463
open market operation	518
open-end fund	653
operating cash flow	262
operating income	254

operating lease	283	private placement	330
operating synergy	433	probability of default	368
operational risk	510	procyclicality	514
option	629	producer price index	49
output gap	23	profit taking	688
outstanding loan	352	progressive tax rate	225
overdraft loan	357	project finance	342
over-the-counter market	547	property and casualty insurance	192
owner's equity	234	public debt	203
		public fund	527

P

parent company	276	public pension	186
passive investment	677	purchasing power parity	113
pass-through certificate	395	put option	637
pay-off	166	puttable bond	598
pension reform	189		

Q

per capita GDP	13	quantitative easing	526

R

petrodollar	86	rate of return	695
petroleum industry	439	rating agency	373
Pfandbrief	623	rating downgrade	377
pharmaceutical industry	438	rating upgrade	376
Phillips curve	46	real asset	67
plain vanilla	635	real estate	178
plant asset	240	real estate industry	450
Plaza Accord	119	real estate investment trust	662
poison pill	424	real exchange rate	105
positive yield	490	real GDP	15
preferred stock	566	real interest rate	488
pre-tax profit	257	recession	31
price earnings ratio	310	recourse loan	171
price stability	51	regional bank	476
price-book value ratio	311	reinsurance	196
primary balance	202	renminbi	138
primary market	455	repo rate	543
prime rate	353		
principal	687		
private equity fund	669		

reserve ratio	522
reserve requirement	521
residential investment	19
residential mortgage-backed securities	393
retail banking	366
retail industry	449
retained earnings	248
return on asset	295
return on equity	296
reverse mortgage	174
rights issue	331
rights offer	326
risk free rate	494
risk premium	690
risk tolerance	691
risk weighted asset	509
Russian ruble	145

S

safe-haven currency	132
sales revenue	249
Samurai bond	600
Sarbanes-Oxley Act	406
saving rate	162
savings account	163
seasoned equity offering	329
secondary market	456
sector fund	655
secured bond	604
secured debt	167
securities company	480
securities market	545
securitization	381
securitized product	382
self-financing	344
selling operation	520
selling, general, and administrative expenses	252
separately managed account	657
services industry	451
share repurchase	337
shareholders' meeting	339
Sharpe ratio	700
short selling	553
short-term bond	606
short-term interest rate	493
single currency	149
small-cap stock	569
social insurance	182
social security expenditure	205
solvency margin	515
South African rand	140
sovereign risk	471
sovereign wealth fund	670
special drawing right	81
speculative grade	379
speculative trading	686
spin-off	428
split rating	380
spot market	111
Stability and Growth Pact	152
stable growth	27
stable shareholder	340
stagflation	59
stagnation	33
state ownership	485
statement of cash flows	231
statement of comprehensive income	269
statutory merger	408
steel industry	440
sterilized intervention	122
stock exchange	546

stock investment trust	649
stock market	564
stock option	401
stock price	574
stock split	327
stock swap	417
stock transfer	418
straight bond	589
strategic alliance	430
structured bond	593
subordinated debt	503
subprime mortgage crisis	9
subsidiary	277
super-long bond	609
supplementary budget	201
swap	628
swap rate	492
swaption	642
Swiss franc	147
syndicated loan	360
systemic risk	513

T

tax reform	227
tax revenue	214
tax system	213
tender offer	419
term loan	358
textile industry	436
third-sector insurance	194
TIBOR	497
tight monetary policy	524
time deposit	164
time-weighted rate of return	698
TOPIX	579
tracking stock	345
trade barrier	94
trade credit	332
trade deficit	93
trade friction	97
trade imbalance	96
trade surplus	92
trade volume	88
trading cost	550
trading limit	560
trading partner	89
transportation industry	446
Treasury bill	617
Treasury bond	619
Treasury note	618
treasury stock	338
triangular merger	410
trust bank	477
turnover period	299
turnover ratio	298

U

UK pound sterling	146
uncollaterized overnight call	541
underwriter	555
unemployment rate	43
universal banking	364
unlisted securities	549
unsecured bond	605
unsecured debt	168
unsterilized intervention	123
US dollar	141

V

value at risk	473
value fund	661
variable annuity	173
variable cost	304
venture capital fund	668

vertical integration	421
vertical merger	414
Volcker Rule	505
voting right	576

W

WACC	316
warrant bond	591
weather derivative	647
white knight	425
wholesale banking	365
wholesale industry	448
working capital	265
work-sharing	405
World Bank	82
World Trade Organization	102

Y

yield curve	489
yield spread	615
yield to maturity	611

Z

zero coupon bond	596
zero interest rate policy	533

索　引（和文）　※数字はセンテンスの番号

アルファベット

ABCP（資産担保コマーシャルペーパー）	387
ABL（資産担保融資）	386
ABS（資産担保証券）	385
BPS（1株当り純資産）	309
BRICs	84
CBO（社債担保証券）	390
CDO（債務担保証券）	388
CLO（ローン担保証券）	389
CMBS（商業不動産担保証券）	394
CMO（不動産抵当証券担保債券）	391
DIPファイナンス	343
EBITDA	259
ECB政策金利	544
EMS（欧州通貨制度）	150
EMU（欧州経済通貨同盟）	151
EPS（1株当り利益）	308
ESOP（従業員持株制度）	402
ETF（上場投資信託）	658
FFレート（フェデラルファンドレート）	542
FOMC（米国連邦公開市場委員会）	529
FTSE100種総合株価指数	581
GDPデフレーター	50
GDP成長	22
IFRS（国際財務報告基準）	268
IMF（国際通貨基金）	80
IPO（新規株式公開）	328
IRR（内部収益率）	318
ITバブル	7
J-REIT（日本型不動産投資信託）	663
Jカーブ	126
LBO（レバレッジドバイアウト）	432
LDI（年金債務重視の運用）	400
LIBOR	496
M&A	407
MBO（マネジメントバイアウト）	431
MBS（不動産担保証券）	392
MMF（マネーマーケットファンド）	665
MMF（マネーマネージメントファンド）	664
NPV（正味現在価値）	317
PBR（株価純資産倍率）	311
PER（株価収益率）	310
RMBS（住宅ローン担保証券）	393
ROA（総資産利益率）	295
ROE（自己資本利益率）	296
SDR（特別引出し権）	81
SEO（公募増資）	329
SMA（ラップ口座）	657
TIBOR	497
Tノート	618
WACC（加重平均資本コスト）	316

あ

アクティブ運用	676
アジア通貨危機	6
アンダーライター	555
安定株主	340
安定成長	27
安定成長協定	152
イールドカーブ	489
イスラム金融	85

イベントドリブンファンド	675
医薬品業界	438
医療費	161
医療保険	183
イングランド銀行	538
インサイダー取引	561
インターバンク市場	462
インタレストカバレッジレシオ	294
インデックスファンド	651
インフレ	52
インフレ圧力	56
インフレヘッジ	57
インフレ目標政策	58
インフレ率	53
インフレ連動債	592
受取手形	237
失われた10年	4
売出	333
売上原価	250
売上総利益	251
売上総利益率	297
売上高	249
売りオペ	520
売掛金	238
運転資金	265
運輸業界	446
運用実績	694
営業外収益	255
営業外費用	256
営業キャッシュフロー	262
営業権（のれん）	280
営業利益	254
英ポンド	146
エクイティファイナンス	321
円高	124
円建て外債	600
オイルダラー	86
黄金株	426
欧州債務危機	11
欧州中央銀行	539
大型株	567
オープンエンド型ファンド	653
オープン市場	463
オフショア市場	466
オフショア通貨取引	134
オプション	629
オペレーショナルリスク	510
オペレーティングリース	283
親会社	276
オルタナティブ投資	680
卸売業界	448

か

買いオペ	519
外貨	130
買掛金	244
外貨準備高	76
外国為替市場	103
外国為替証拠金取引	646
外国為替取引	107
外国人持株比率	583
介護保険	184
外需	25
回転期間	299
回転率	298
外部格付	375
開放経済	100
化学業界	437
格上げ	376
格下げ	377
格付機関	373
確定給付型年金	398
確定拠出年金	399
額面	614

貸渋り	363	ンス)	396
貸付残高	352	企業年金	397
可処分所得	157	企業物価指数	48
家電業界	444	議決権	576
カナダドル	142	基軸通貨	131
株価	574	規制緩和	500
株式移転	418	既存店ベースの売上高	42
株式公開買付け	419	期待リターン	689
株式交換	417	逆イールド	491
株式市場	564	キャッシュフロー	260
株式投資	681	キャッシュフロー計算書	231
株式投資信託	649	キャピタルゲイン	696
株式プレミアム	575	キャピタルロス	697
株式分割	327	キャリートレード	112
株式持合い	346	吸収合併	408
株主資本コスト	315	協調介入	121
株主総会	339	協調融資	360
株主割当発行	331	協調利下げ	534
下方リスク	692	ギルト	620
空売り	553	金価格	66
為替介入	120	銀行借入れ	350
為替ヘッジ	109	銀行制度	351
為替見通し	110	銀行持株会社	479
為替リスク	108	金庫株	338
為替レート	104	緊縮財政政策	211
間接金融	323	金本位制	115
間接税	218	金融監督機関	516
カントリーリスク	470	金融緩和政策	525
元本	687	金融機関	474
関連会社	278	金融危機	10
機械業界	441	金融資産	159
機械受注	39	金融市場	452
機関投資家	683	金融自由化	467
企業価値	312	金融政策	517
企業間信用	332	金融制度改革	501
企業再建	427	金融引締政策	524
企業統治(コーポレートガバナ		金利	486

金利オプション	638	コア Tier1	511
金利先物	630	公開市場操作	518
金利スワップ	633	鉱工業生産	38
金利政策	523	公債	203
金利リスク	469	公正価値	273
クーポン利率	610	厚生年金	188
クラウディングアウト	212	公定歩合	540
グラススティーガル法	504	公的資金	527
クリーンサープラス	285	公的年金	186
繰延税金資産	282	豪ドル	143
クレジットカード	176	購買力平価	113
クレジットデフォルトスワップ（CDS）	644	合弁事業	429
クレジットデリバティブ	643	小売業界	449
クローズドエンド型ファンド	654	コーラブル債	597
軍事費	206	コールオプション	636
景気回復	28	子会社	277
景気拡大	29	小型株	569
景気後退	31	国債	585
景気失速	30	国際収支	68
景気循環	34	国際通貨制度	114
景気循環株	570	国債費	204
景気循環増幅効果	514	国税	215
景気停滞	33	国内総生産	12
景気動向指数	36	国民所得	156
経済指標	26	国民年金	187
経済成長	35	国有化	485
経常収支	69	個人所得税	219
決算発表	267	個人投資家	684
限界収入	306	コストインフレ	54
限界費用	307	固定為替相場制	117
減価償却	253	固定金利住宅ローン	169
現金同等物	236	固定資産税	222
現金配当	334	固定費	305
建設業界	445	固定負債	245
減損損失	274	固定利付債	594
原油価格	65	コマーシャルペーパー	461
		コミットメントライン	359

雇用なき景気回復	8	三角合併	410
雇用保険	185	時価評価額	557
コングロマリット	415	時間加重収益率	698
		直物市場	111

さ

サーキットブレーカー	558	資金不足	465
サービス業界	451	資金余剰	464
サーベンスオクスリー（SOX）法	406	仕組債	593
		自己金融	344
債券価格	613	自己資本（純資産）	234
債権国	73	自己資本比率《一般事業会社》	288
債券先物	632	自己資本比率《金融機関》	508
債券市場	584	資産	232
債券投資信託	650	資産インフレ	55
在庫投資	21	資産運用会社	481
最終利回り	611	資産株	572
歳出	200	資産買収	412
財政赤字	198	資産配分	678
財政黒字	197	自社株買い	337
財政政策	208	市場規制当局	556
最低資本金制度	324	市場リスク	468
最低賃金	404	指数オプション	640
裁定取引	685	システミックリスク	513
歳入	199	失業保険申請件数	44
再保険	196	失業率	43
財務キャッシュフロー	264	実効為替レート	106
債務国	74	実質為替レート	105
財務諸表	228	実質金利	488
債務超過	292	実質GDP	15
財務リスク	291	実物資産	67
最優遇貸出金利	353	質への逃避	693
裁量的財政政策	209	自動車業界	442
先物オプション	641	自動車保険	193
先物契約	627	ジニーメイ	484
先渡契約	626	支払準備率	522
差金決済取引	645	支払手形	243
サブプライム住宅ローン危機	9	私募	330
		資本金	246

資本コスト	313	消費財	99
資本財	98	消費支出	16
資本市場（長期金融市場）	454	消費者金融	175
資本剰余金	247	消費者信頼感指数	37
資本的支出	319	消費者物価指数	47
資本流出	79	消費税	221
資本流入	78	商品価格	64
シャープレシオ	700	食品業界	435
社会保険	182	所得格差	158
社会保障関係費	205	新興市場	83
社債	588	新設合併	409
社債スプレッド	371	信託銀行	477
ジャパンプレミアム	498	人民元	138
ジャンク債	603	信用格付	374
収益見通し	266	信用スプレッド	370
収益率	695	信用取引	577
終身雇用	403	信用与信枠	361
住宅価格	180	信用リスク	369
住宅着工件数	40	スイスフラン	147
住宅着工許可件数	41	垂直合併	414
住宅投資	19	垂直統合	421
自由貿易	101	水平合併	413
需給ギャップ	23	水平統合	420
取得原価	272	スタグフレーション	59
順イールド	490	ストックオプション	401
準備預金	521	スピンオフ	428
商業銀行	475	スプリットレーティング	380
商業用不動産	179	スワップ	628
証券化	381	スワップション	642
証券会社	480	スワップレート	492
証券化商品	382	生活費	160
証券市場	545	税効果会計	281
証券取引所	546	政策金利	535
上場証券	548	生産シナジー	433
証書貸付	355	生産者物価指数	49
少数株主持分	279	税収	214
譲渡性預金	460	税制	213

税制改革	227	棚卸資産（在庫）	239
製造業	434	短期金融市場	453
成長株ファンド	660	短期金利	493
税引後利益	258	短期国債	617
税引前利益	257	短期債	606
政府支出	18	第三分野保険	194
政府保証債	587	団体保険	195
生命保険	191	担保	354
世界銀行	82	担保付債券	604
世界大恐慌	1	地価	181
世界貿易機関	102	地方銀行	476
石油業界	439	地方債	586
セクターファンド	655	地方財政	207
積極財政政策	210	地方税	216
設備稼働率	302	中央銀行	530
設備投資	20	中型株	568
ゼロ金利政策	533	中期債	607
ゼロクーポン債（割引債）	596	超過収益	699
繊維業界	436	長期金利	495
戦略的提携	430	長期債	608
増資	325	超長期債	609
相続税	223	直接金融	322
相場操縦	562	直接税	217
贈与税	224	直接投資	77
その他資本収支	72	貯蓄率	162
ソブリンウェルスファンド	670	通貨オプション	639
ソブリンリスク	471	通貨危機	135
ソルベンシーマージン	515	通貨切下げ	129
損益計算書	230	通貨先物	631
損益分岐点	303	通貨スワップ	634
損害保険	192	通貨スワップ協定	136
		通貨取引	127

た

タームローン	358	通貨変動	128
対外債務	75	強気相場	551
貸借対照表	229	ディーラー	554
ダウ平均株価	580	定期預金	164
		ディスインフレ	61

ディフェンシブ株	571	取引先リスク	372
手形貸付	356	ドルペッグ制	133
敵対的買収	423	ドル安	125
鉄鋼業界	440		
デットエクイティスワップ	347	**な**	
デットファイナンス	320	内需	24
デビットカード	177	ナスダック	582
デフォルト確率	368	二重課税	226
デフレ	62	日経平均株価	578
デフレスパイラル	63	日本円	137
デュアルカレンシー債	601	日本銀行	536
デュレーション	612	日本国債（JGB）	616
デリバティブ（金融派生商品）	624	ニューエコノミー	5
デリバティブ証券	625	値幅制限	560
転換社債型新株予約権付社債	590	年金制度改革	189
電気電子業界	443	ノンバンク	482
天候デリバティブ	647	ノンリコースローン	172
店頭市場	547		
電力業界	447	**は**	
統一通貨	149	バーゼル基準	507
投機的格付	379	バイアウトファンド	667
投機取引	686	買収	411
当座貸越	357	配当性向	336
当座比率	287	配当利回り	335
当座預金	459	ハイパーインフレ	60
投資キャッシュフロー	263	ハイブリッド証券	348
投資銀行	478	バスケット取引	559
投資銀行業務	367	パススルー証書	395
投資支出	17	発行市場	455
投資収支	71	パッシブ運用	677
投資信託	648	バブル経済	3
投資適格	378	バランスファンド	652
投資適格債	602	バリューアットリスク	473
東証株価指数	579	販売費および一般管理費	252
ドッドフランク法	506	非関税障壁	95
トラッキングストック	345	非上場証券	549
取引コスト	550	1人当りGDP	13

避難通貨	132	分散投資	679
非農業部門雇用者数	45	ブンズ	621
非不胎化介入	123	ペイオフ	166
ファイアウォール	502	米長期国債	619
ファイナンスリース	284	米ドル	141
ファクタリング	384	ヘッジファンド	666
ファニーメイ	483	変額年金	173
ファンダメンタル分析	682	ベンチャーキャピタルファンド	668
ファンドオブファンズ	659	変動為替相場制	118
ファンドブリーフ	623	変動金利住宅ローン	170
フィリップス曲線	46	変動費	304
不況	32	変動利付債	595
負債	233	ポイズンピル	424
負債コスト	314	貿易	87
負債比率（D/E レシオ）	289	貿易相手国	89
不胎化介入	122	貿易赤字	93
普通株	565	貿易黒字	92
普通社債	589	貿易収支	70
普通預金	163	貿易障壁	94
物価安定	51	貿易不均衡	96
プッタブル債	598	貿易摩擦	97
プットオプション	637	貿易量	88
不動産	178	包括利益	270
不動産業界	450	包括利益計算書	269
不動産抵当証券	622	法人税	220
不動産投資信託	662	ホールセールバンキング	365
プライベートエクイティファンド	669	簿価	271
プライマリーバランス	202	保険会社	190
プラザ合意	119	補正予算	201
ブラジルレアル	144	ボルカールール	505
ブラックマンデー	2	ホワイトナイト	425
フリーキャッシュフロー	261	香港ドル	139
不良債権	362		
プレーンバニラ	635	**ま**	
ブレトンウッズ体制	116	マーケットタイミング	674
プロジェクトファイナンス	342	マーケットニュートラル	673
		マネージドフューチャーズ	671

マネーストック(マネーサプライ)	457
マネーロンダリング	563
マネタリーベース	458
南アフリカランド	140
ミューチュアルファンド	656
無形固定資産	241
無担保コール翌日物	541
無担保債	605
無担保債務	168
無リスク金利	494
名目金利	487
名目GDP	14
メインバンク	341
メザニンファイナンス	383
持株会社	416

や

有形固定資産	240
友好的買収	422
融資業務	349
優先株	566
有担保債務	167
有利子負債	293
優良株	573
ユーロ	148
ユーロ円債	599
ユーロカレンシー	153
ユーロ市場	155
ユーロダラー	154
輸出依存度	90
ユニバーサルバンキング	364
輸入依存度	91
預金保険	165
弱気相場	552

ら

ライツオファリング（新株予約権無償割当て）	326
利上げ	531
利益剰余金	248
利食い	688
リコースローン	171
利下げ	532
リスクアセット	509
リスク許容度	691
リスクプレミアム	690
リテールバンキング	366
リバースモーゲージ	174
利回り格差	615
流通市場	456
流動資産	235
流動性の罠	499
流動性バッファー	512
流動性リスク	472
流動比率	286
流動負債	242
量的金融緩和	526
累進税率	225
劣後債務	503
レバレッジ比率	290
レポレート	543
連結財務諸表	275
連邦準備制度理事会	537
労働生産性	300
労働分配率	301
ロシアルーブル	145
ロングショートファンド	672

わ

ワークシェアリング	405
ワラント債	591
割引窓口貸出	528
割安株ファンド	661

■著者略歴■

砺波　元（となみ　げん）
1968年12月25日生まれ。
1991年3月　東京大学経済学部卒業。
1991年4月　㈱日本興業銀行入行。
日系大手金融機関グループにて、国内外の金融教育・投資教育に関する業務に従事。
学生時代より英語教育の方法論や効率的な英語学習法にも関心をもち、当時の構想が本書の原型となった。
2004〜2006年　早稲田大学ビジネス情報アカデミー講師。
㈳日本証券アナリスト協会検定会員。

［おもな著書］
『資産運用のパフォーマンス測定』（2000年、金融財政事情研究会）
『基礎から学べる投資・運用関連数式集』（2003年、金融財政事情研究会）
『ファンドマネジメントのすべて』（共著：2007年、東京書籍）

KINZAIバリュー叢書
金融英文700選

平成25年4月24日　第1刷発行

著　者　砺　波　　　元
発行者　倉　田　　　勲
印刷所　三松堂印刷株式会社

〒160-8520　東京都新宿区南元町19
発　行　所　一般社団法人　金融財政事情研究会
編集部　TEL 03(3355)2251　FAX 03(3357)7416
販　　売　株式会社きんざい
販売受付　TEL 03(3358)2891　FAX 03(3358)0037
URL http://www.kinzai.jp/

・本書の内容の一部あるいは全部を無断で複写・複製・転訳載すること、および磁気または光記録媒体、コンピュータネットワーク上等へ入力することは、法律で認められた場合を除き、著作者および出版社の権利の侵害となります。
・落丁・乱丁本はお取替えいたします。定価はカバーに表示してあります。

ISBN978-4-322-12320-3